ADVANCE PRAISE FOR

"*A Culture of Refusal* takes a closer look at the social circumstances that nurture adolescent behavior by exploring young people's unique language—a language that is not only the gateway to understanding one's culture, but also one's perception of oneself and others. Here, Blake cultivates the sensitivities of the reader and changes our hearts in terms of how we perceive young people who are culturally and linguistically diverse in today's society."

—*David Ciampi, Director of the Forensic Group, New York City,*
and Author of The Ecology of Youth Violence

Joseph L. DeVitis & Linda Irwin-DeVitis
GENERAL EDITORS

Vol. 15

PETER LANG
New York • Washington, D.C./Baltimore • Bern
Frankfurt am Main • Berlin • Brussels • Vienna • Oxford

Brett Elizabeth Blake

THE Lives AND Literacies
OF Out-of-School Adolescents

PETER LANG
New York • Washington, D.C./Baltimore • Bern
Frankfurt am Main • Berlin • Brussels • Vienna • Oxford

Library of Congress Cataloging-in-Publication Data

Blake, Brett Elizabeth.
A culture of refusal: the lives and literacies of out-of-school adolescents /
Brett Elizabeth Blake.
p. cm. — (Adolescent cultures, school and society; v. 15)
Includes bibliographical references.
1. Youth with social disabilities—Education (Secondary)—United States—Case studies.
2. Child migrant agricultural laborers—Education (Secondary)—United States—
Case studies. 3. Dropouts—United States—Case studies. 4. Non-formal education—
United States—Case studies. 5. Critical pedagogy—United States—Case studies.
I. Title. II. Adolescent cultures, school & society; v. 15.
LC4069.4.B42   373.12'913—dc21   99046199
ISBN 0-8204-4871-0
ISSN 1091-1464

Die Deutsche Bibliothek-CIP-Einheitsaufnahme

Blake, Brett Elizabeth:
A culture of refusal: the lives and literacies of out-of-school adolescents /
Brett Elizabeth Blake.
—New York; Washington, D.C./Baltimore; Bern;
Frankfurt am Main; Berlin; Brussels; Vienna; Oxford: Lang.
(Adolescent cultures, school & society; Vol. 15)
ISBN 0-8204-4871-0

Cover design by Sophie Boorsch Appel

The paper in this book meets the guidelines for permanence and durability
of the Committee on Production Guidelines for Book Longevity
of the Council of Library Resources.

© 2004 Peter Lang Publishing, Inc., New York
275 Seventh Avenue, 28th Floor, New York, NY 10001
www.peterlangusa.com

Printed in the United States of America

This one is for the "girlfriends"

To Carol, my mother; Grace, my beloved, late grandmother; Blondie, Pillow, and Corona, my "babies" and of course Joanne Robertson, Maureen Daw, Josephine Galliher, Grace Ibanez Friedman, Barbara Nelson, Stephanie Kuhn, Colleen Lonigan, Esther Denaro Maltese, Bunty Ethington, Judy Stern Torres, Shirley Steinberg, Eva Roca, Anne Mungai, Nancy Adler, Judi Lester, Joyce Mizerak, Laura Leeper, Linda Pickering, Kathy Grasso, and all the mothers and educators who have worked tirelessly, often with little or no pay, to help make the lives and hence, the literacies, of all children, more peaceful and more hopeful.

TABLE OF CONTENTS

FOREWORD

The book for which I'm privileged to write the foreword is about rebellion. It is about the rebellion of the author, Brett Blake, as well as the experience of rebellion by others in our society. Dr. Blake's rebellion is against the century–long history in Western research and literature that has established parameters, glamorized, and mythologized adolescence. She seeks to uncover the essence of adolescent populations who have been marginalized and viewed as the "others." Her journey takes her beyond a postmodernist critique of the "Other" and in doing so the others, in a very real sense, become the authors of the book and, through their own literacies, illuminate the "culture of refusal."

When adolescence emerged during the 18th century in industrial Europe and North America as a discrete phase of development writers—most notably philosopher Jean-Jacques Rousseau—began to trace and understand it as an era of dramatic physical and intellectual change and great emotional upheaval. The representation of society as antagonistic to adolescence is at the heart of Rousseau's work. But more fundamentally, society is viewed as the corrupting force to the natural innocence of the adolescent. As time has gone on, how this relationship is viewed is an organizing aspect of how adolescence, itself, is written about. At the turn of the 20th century, for example, adolescents were depicted by writers as vulnerable to their own emotional lives and the demands of the society around them, experiencing inner turmoil and social awkwardness. At times, they were seen as against social norms, challenging, and searching. The Futurists celebrated youth and adolescence, rejecting the artistic and social norms of adults. And Freud portrayed the conflict at an individual level between adolescent drives and social conscience.

Fifty years later, the adolescent was described as "alienated," feeling her/his life is meaningless and that there is little control over events. This portrayal in literature and scholarly work has achieved the status of a familiar cultural icon. Alienation became associated with the adolescent quest for identity, constructed as a distrust of adults, a rejection of their values, and a pessimistic world view. With the social activism of many adolescents of the 1960s, "self–alienation" began to appear as characterizations of them. And in recent years, the alienation of the adolescent has become part of what is seen as "normal" development, a deliberate identity choice, a choice to withdraw from groups formally identified with.

Yet in this increasingly interiorized view of adolescent refusal, the social and cultural settings are largely obscured. Writers create images of adolescents as self–absorbed and egocentric, making decisions by impulse and, withdrawn from societal conflict, preferring the conflict of peer groups and gangs. What they often don't address is the communities and social environments in which they are self–absorbed—or self–protective—and impulsive—or quick–witted. Our understanding of their environments becomes even more necessary as literature and scholarship continue to expand to other cultures and other cultural groups.

As the writings on alienation in Western societies developed, the research of adolescents in other cultures began to expand as well. Writers then compared other cultures to our own, resulting in the construction of dichotomies, such as individualistic/independent (Western) versus collectivistic/interdependence (non–Western) to explain why adolescent rebellion isn't a universal phenomenon. But recent research has suggested that these dichotomies co–exist to an extent in all cultures. And when these other cultures enter into our own, the adolescent/social conflict takes on ethnic, linguistic, or racial meanings that become more challenging: how can the same lens be used to understand adolescent lives when each community has its own understanding of adolescence?

But we continue to do so. We construct the "Other" and keep adolescents' communities and their voices silent; out of our gaze. And constructions of the "Other" becomes part of our pedagogy. Adolescent novels have been integrated into curriculum in many schools with the educational claim that doing so facilitates development. Through reading about "others" and their perspectives, educators hope to help them to gain "self" acceptance, the ability to cope with the shift from parental control to societal demands, and become more mature thinkers. From a postmodern view, the questions that should be raised are about the "voices" involved in this activity (the teacher's, author's, and the students') as well as whose voice is being "heard." Does an adult author offering a fictionalized account of an adolescent's life speak the language of adolescent readers—particularly those who are marginalized? In many respects, a postmodern critique held out the promise that we would have to look at our "othering" of adolescents as we write texts to each other rather than listening to their voices and involving them in the conversation. Unfortunately—and something that Dr. Blake clearly recognizes—the discourse of postmodernism does not escape its own critique. The postmodernist continues to write to us about "them," continuing to make them the object of study.

One could argue that creating a "we–other" or "us–them" dichotomy is a false one that merely reinforces divisions; that most adolescent voices merge with those in power without any connection to a culture of refusal. While this is a valuable discussion, the groups that are the focus of Dr. Blake's book are clearly divided from us. Any power that they might have to speak is taken away by their status. And, having described their status, the author rightly allows them to do just that: speak. And in the process, they begin to demystify their experience within the social and cultural settings of their lives. The implications for "us" who read her work and are in positions to allow these young people to speak are far–reaching and challenging. And the effort to understand the culture of refusal is a powerful journey that is well worth taking.

Devin G. Thornburg, Ph.D.
Director, Metropolitan Center
Steinhardt School of Education
New York University

ACKNOWLEDGMENTS

I gratefully acknowledge the staff at Peter Lang Publishing, particularly the very fine editorial assistance of Peter Lang's editor for this series, Joe DeVitis; the patience of both the managing director, Chris Myers and the production coordinator, Sophie Appel; and the friendship and support of the education editor, Shirley Steinberg. A special thanks to George Mungai who tirelessly worked through the many camera-ready changes.

Thank you, too, to the members of my department at St. John's University, especially Robert Allen. As a graduate assistant, he was invaluable as a reader and critic of my work, reminding me ever–so gently what it really means to be black in America. I know his insights will help him to change the injustices he so rightly sees and feels every day.

A loving thank you to Charlie Galliher. Coming "out of the darkness into the light" is a wonderful place to begin a journey, especially with him.

And finally, this book would have never been completed without the constant attention and encouragement of my father, Robert W. Blake, professor emeritus, State University of New York, who truly believed I could finish this project (and do it well) amidst increasingly complex roles as an educator and a single parent of an adolescent. As in the words of our nation's new chairman for the National Endowment for the Arts (NEA), Dana Gioia, Dad, you too deserve "sonnets in folio" rather than this "meager prose."

Portions of Chapter Five were previously printed in "Fruit of the Devil: Writing & English Language Learners," by Brett Elizabeth Blake, *Language Arts* 78, No.5, May 2001. © National Council of Teachers of English. Reprinted with permission.

Chapter One

Introduction

There has been a demonization of youth, particularly young people of color, who are stereotypically protrayed as roaming the streets and destroying the fabric of society (Stein, Katz, Madriz, & Shick, 1977, p.2).

Hey, Chicago lady! Do you know who Bugsy Malone was? yells Sam, a 17–year–old African–American kid doing time for drug trafficking and weapons possession. Sam and I began what would turn out to be a long, and on–going, discussion about gangsters, Chicago, Michael Jordan, and his home and school life. "I really liked school", he tells me, "and most of my teachers, but outside everyone's talking about fast money...money is nice...you got to be able to provide." (Fieldnotes, 1/28/98).

Adolescents who are shut out from the public space that most of us operate in on a daily basis, who are "demonized" by a society that believes that minority youth, in particular, will take over entire cities, leaving destruction in their wake—those adolescents who are shut out of the *central* public space in which they are supposed to be equal participants in their social and literate selves—school—find their own public spaces in which to live and to become "literate." These public, cultural spaces operate outside of the classroom and are deeply embedded in an alternative culture—the culture of refusal (Covington, 1997, p. 126).

The culture of refusal operates on the premise that there is little possibility for youth in a society that disdains and distrusts the poor, especially if the poor are also persons of color. The culture of refusal erodes any sense of hope, channeling anger and disappointment into "non–participation." Poor youth of color realize this sense more acutely, as they are routinely marginalized both in and out–of–school. As a result, these marginalized adolescents "refuse" to be part of the mainstream culture at all, reflecting this refusal throughout all aspects of their lives, including how they choose to learn and become literate.

When I moved to upstate New York from Chicago several years ago to continue my work as a teacher educator, I was shocked to learn that many of the schools there experienced similar challenges that I had seen schools struggling with in Chicago, including high dropout rates, low expectations by teachers and administrators, violence in the schools, and a general apathy and belief that these young people could not, and would not, learn.[1] I had not expected to see these kinds of issues in a district that was much smaller, thereby appearing more controlled and contained, I thought, from the damaging effects of a large, urban system that was, in many senses, spinning out of control.

In fact, though, the issues that the schools in upstate New York were dealing with were *so similar*, that the local paper ran a series of articles comparing the two school districts. Called, "Classroom crackdown: Chicago tries tough approach to turn its schools around" (1998) the series targeted the "educational failure" found in both Chicago and upstate New York, citing a lack of "kicking a little ass" as a major reason for the potential "demise" of these school districts. In my reply to the newspaper (Blake, B. E. (1998, April 9). *Give city students flight instruction*. [Letter to the Editor]. The Democrat & Chronicle, p. A12.) I chronicled several events and examples from my own experience in both school districts that spoke to the successes of urban, public education, rather than to its failure. This book is about success of a different sort. It is about those so–called "marginalized" adolescents who, for many reasons, have found themselves engulfed in a "culture of refusal" as they drop out of school and the public spaces that would afford them the opportunities to become successful. These students' asses were not just kicked a little. These students' asses were kicked a lot, and the further they strayed from the mainstream public spaces in which success is bred in traditional ways, the more ass–kicking they received. Success to these adolescents comes at the ultimate price— they are either locked–out or locked–up, as school and society become metaphors for who and what they cannot be—where they didn't and never will belong, but where they know they must return to become successful in the "traditional" way.

The focus of this book is on the lives and literacies of migrant field workers and incarcerated youth; a set of what Ayers (Blake, 1997, xii) would call, "multiply-marginalized" youth. Poor, of color, often second language learning, these are the adolescents who, feared by most and described by few, have either dropped out of school, plan to drop out of school, or have been "dropped" from school, in order to work in the fields or the streets to earn money. It is here in the fields and the streets, and ultimately, in the jails, that multiply-marginalized youth live and develop their own lives and literacies within their own cultural space.

---

[1]This is not to say there were not wonderful teachers and wonderful classrooms in upstate New York. There were plenty and I will be talking about two of them in particular in Chapters Eight and Nine of this book.

What can these adolescents tell us about school and society? What can we learn about youth who develop their own forms of literacy and success? How does the culture of refusal work among these youth? And what does this culture tell us about schools, about how to change schools, and about how to affect change throughout society? These are among the questions this book will seek to explore, as it seeks to describe the lives and literacies of these youth themselves.

Overview of the Book

Chapter 2 addresses more fully the rationale behind my beginning this project among this particular group of adolescents. It highlights how I struggled on many levels with figuring out how to represent these adolescents as they wished to be seen: as good, decent, kids who had made "mistakes" along the way, but who had suffered gravely from the inescapable racism and poverty that engulfed and consumed them. Through critical race theory and feminist inquiry, I examine not only issues of access, reporting, and representation, but also of analysis, particularly around making statements and interpretations of kids whom I call the quintessential "Other."

Chapter 3 explores more closely the literature concerning adolescents and adolescent culture. Adolescence, representing roughly the ages of 13 to 19, is the period in children's lives when they begin to separate from the adult world and start to identify with their peer world. It is also a time when students begin to separate their formal education from other more, perhaps, powerful learning experiences outside the classroom. But, because formal education has traditionally focused on autonomy and independence, whereas the needs of adolescents are group acceptance and dependence, it is a precarious time for adolescents and schooling. This phenomenon becomes even more complex and compelling as it is intertwined with race, class, gender, and language within a culture of refusal.

In Chapter 4, I discuss the theoretical underpinnings of Brian Street's (1995) term "local literacies." Street proposes that the notion of literacy has not been problematized sufficiently, so that in general only one form of literacy is acknowledged and accepted. This literacy is framed, he asserts, from within "the particular textual interpretative processes currently being canonized" (Kell, 1997, p. 242). Both Street (1995) and Kell (1997) reject this "autonomous model of literacy" for "local literacies" that are grounded in specific local practices, and do not attempt to hide or "disguise cultural and ideological assumptions." Developing and acknowledging marginalized adolescents' local literacies may be one powerful way in which to help both them and teachers to break the culture of refusal.

Chapters 5 and 6 begin the descriptive part of this book. Here, I explore and describe the particular contexts in which the migrant and incarcerated adolescents lived, worked, and went to school. Traditional stories are heard not only of their "failures" and of their "rehabilitations" (e.g., school as rehab), but also of their perceived successes from a wide variety of sources including the media, parents, teachers, and the general public. In Chapter 7, these adolescents break out of their culture of refusal and talk and write about themselves, situating their lives through their own personal and cultural, that is, local literacies.

In Chapters 8 and 9, I ask two upstate New York teachers to reflect and write about the unique and successful practices and perspectives that they brought to their classrooms. Stephanie Kuhn, an urban ESL, Option III ("severely emotionally disturbed," as designated by New York State) teacher; and Colleen Lonigan, an adult migrant educator and ESL teacher and program coordinator, remind us, in the words of Ayers (1993), that teaching is after all, "primarily a matter of love."

In Chapter 10 I sketch out methods and techniques that I believe can directly "help" teachers to find ways to engage these multiply–marginalized adolescents in school–related literacy tasks. Here, I not only discuss classroom–based teacher inquiry, but also the "exemplary" practices I have seen teachers use as a result of their own inquiry. Further, future directions are sketched out as to the notion of the "culture of refusal" vis–à–vis new "Standards" being required on state and national levels (already approved in New York State) designed to further canonize certain sets of literacy practices.

And, finally, I discuss the very real loss of these multiply–marginalized adolescents while asking, "What may be the effect of this loss on schooling, on families, on society in general?" Through a review of my previous work on urban adolescents as well as my work here, I compare and contrast the literature and my observations, drawing important implications: girls' voices have been muted and silenced; boys' hearts have been destroyed.

Summary

Perspectives of youth and, "the ways in which they attach meaning to their lives [and literacies]...is not a common focus in the educational literature" Phelan, Davidson, & Yu, 1998, p. 17). The contextualization of these youths' lives, however, provides a broadened view of the ways in which they worked within a "culture of refusal" to design their own spaces and places of learning to live and to become literate.

A knowledge and understanding of these youths' lives and literacies is important if we are to find ways in which to provide these youths with opportunities to make their own choices: choices that acknowledge the cultural imprints they carry, choices that make us all richer and broaden all of our lives and literacies as they broaden theirs as well. By developing and acknowledging these adolescents' local, out–of–school literacies, we, as teachers and teacher educators, help to break the culture of refusal of our students *in school*. By doing so, we provide them with schools and classrooms that are equitable and challenging, where they want to come and learn, and where they, too, can express their lives and literacies without us "refusing" them.

Chapter Two

Rationale, Contexts, and Methodology
Issues of Access and Studying the Other

I think we should be scrutinizing the values of the powerful...I'm going to suggest that we start a think tank where the poor can be hired to figure out the pa-
thologies of the rich and recommend some behavioral conditioning to improve
them...I think that would be a far more interesting study than another book about
the underclass (Kozol, in Kirsch, 1999, p.61).

Feminism and Critical Race Theory

This study situates the lives and literacies of multiply–marginalized
adolescents in a larger context of feminist inquiry embedded within
critical race theory. Central to this approach is a focus on voice, silence, reflection, and action (Belenky, Clinchy, Goldberger, & Tarule,
1986; Brown & Gilligan, 1992; Rogers, 1993) notions that could not be
completely captured and expressed by feminist inquiry alone. Rather, the
analysis of how deeply and profoundly race, ethnicity, class, and gender
shape perceptions, assumptions, and expectations, a central tenet of critical
race theory, was used not only to guide the feminist inquiry, but also to
help apply the insights gained from the inquiry itself.

Inherent in feminist inquiry is the premise that there are other intellectual capacities and experiences valued by oppressed groups that do not appear in the current standard measures. Research methodologies that seek to
embrace a feminist perspective, then, include personal experiences as
"standard," seeking to uncover and discover:

> the epistemological value of using [one's] experiences as resources for discovering new
> theory. Instead of simply validating or uncovering scientific truths' about mainstream
> cultures, feminist research asks questions that lead to changes in oppressed conditions,
> usually those of women, but that can also apply to men and children in underpowered
> life roles (Hollingsworth, 1992, p. 376).

A critical race approach attempts to locate these experiences firmly at
"the intersection of race, class, and gender...so as to decenter and *complicate...*" (emphasis mine) the underlying issues of race, for example, even
further (Fine & Weis, 1998, p. 440). That is, a critical race approach ne-

cessitates a deeper "probing" of not only Others' experiences, but of one's own experiences as well:

> to narrate the experience…to unearth the voices of people usually not heard and to excavate these voices across a wide range of life's activities. (p. 436)

A critical race approach does indeed complicate feminist approaches. For example, Harding (1987) suggests that there are three distinguishing features of any feminist analysis. The first suggests that such an analysis of race, class, and gender must be considered in the "plural," rather than making an assumption or a conclusion based on a single experience. These plural experiences become the new theoretical and empirical resources from which we should conduct and make sense of our research. The second, suggests that "the purposes of research and analysis [should not be] separable from the origins of the research problems" (p. 8). In other words, feminist inquiry should be conducted "for," not just "on," marginalized groups, so that these groups are in the position to potentially benefit from the research *outcomes*. The third criterion simply states that the researcher must be on "the same critical plane as the overt subject matter" (p. 8), that is, a member of the same group being studied.   Critical race theory provides a crucial analytical tool for understanding the imbalances and hence the inequity in conducting research on those not from the "same critical plane." Feminist inquiry, at least according to Harding, would posit that I, for example, as a white, middle–class college professor, could not accurately represent and describe a study of multiply–marginalized adolescents. Critical race theory, on the other hand, puts forth the position that because the deep inequity is there, both on a group and individual level, we must "get at" it, and in doing so, we should "refuse essentialisms of race, class, and gender…[as we] recognize enormous variation…[so as to] recognize that the intersections [of race, class, and gender…can lead] to important questions and generalizations" (Fine & Weis, 1998, p. 440). From this position, then, it became possible for me to understand, at least theoretically, how deeply the adolescents' experiences were "classed, raced, ethnicized, and gendered" (p. 437), thereby helping me to further recognize, and represent, how profoundly polarized our perceptions, experiences, and differences were; how dramatic the "discursive departures" of our respective lives had not only been socially constructed but deeply engraved and ingrained in society today (p. 455).

This issue, in fact, became central to my representation of these adolescents; how I inescapably described them as the "Other" as I struggled with portraying their lives and literacies as they wished them to be portrayed.

(See further discussion of this below, under "Access and Representation".)

Oral History and Autobiography

Critical race theory has also provided this study with a framework that not only helps to analyze the adolescents' lives and literacies, but also to challenge how the specific techniques of oral history and autobiography, used here to gather voices, have traditionally held up these voices against a dominant standard. Here, as feminist inquiry underscores my continued, deep commitment to using oral history and autobiographical techniques in "drawing on women's daily lives as a resource for analyzing society" (Frankenberg, 1993, p. 32), critical race theory helps me both to learn to apply or "map" these resources onto broader social contexts (Frankenberg, 1993, p. 6), and to learn to reshape and redefine how these techniques can be better used.

According to Gluck & Patai (1991), although oral history was originally used as a way of recovering voices of suppressed groups, it did not, at the same time, serve the interests of these groups well (p. 1). Essentially, oral history methodologies did not represent suppressed groups in their own languages or voices. That is, these groups' experiences often lay beyond the current "constraints of acceptable discourse" (Heilbrun, 1988, p. 11), reflected through language that was detailed and emotional; constructed from, often, private and personal spaces that were socially and culturally unacceptable. Oral histories, for example, revealed the "distinct imbalances in power and privilege" (Gluck & Patai, 1991, p. 3) characterized by linguistic patterns different from the standard. Stories of those who were marginalized, therefore, were always problematic when analyzed by a dominant standard of discourse. Autobiography, too, although acknowledged as a methodology that allows for oppressed voices, has been criticized for the kinds of discourse these voices have produced. Like oral history, autobiography has been judged against a dominant standard that does not acknowledge certain non–standard linguistic features such as emotion and detail. Further, autobiography is often seen as "narcissistic" and unbalanced (Jipson, Munro, Victor, Froude–Jones, & Freed–Rowland, 1995), particularly when it is seen as helping people to make sense of their lives.

Both critical race approaches and feminist analyses have sought to steady this imbalance by listening to these stories against a non–dominant standard. Here, gender, race, and language become "basic units" of study and analysis as people are urged to tell stories in their own terms. The discourse becomes one that is better attuned to the more immediate realities of [one's] personal experience (Andersen & Jack, 1991) rather than "one [that is] framed [to] reflect men's dominant positions in the culture" (p. 11).

Essentially this shift requires not only that gender, race, class, and language be the "standard" units of study and analysis, but that a new set of questions be embedded within the "standard." Further, the "processes of analysis should be suspended or at least subordinated to the processes of listening" in exploring themes or emergent patterns in these stories. And finally, linguistic features need to be seen as potentially problematic as language shapes and reshapes not only the way stories are told and who listens to them, but also the very representation of self and identity.

In the next section, I set the stage for an understanding of where, and how, that is, under what conditions, these adolescents lived. Here, I begin to describe the broader physical and emotional contexts in which these youth explored and developed their literate selves. Framed by my perceptions as an adolescent growing up in upstate New York, and supported by various statistical information, I explain why these adolescents have gone so unnoticed, and thereby why a study of their lives and literacies is so crucial. Finally, from there, I discuss issues of access, representation, and data analysis, specifically as to the particular challenges that both critical race theory and feminist inquiry demand of such a discussion.

Rationale and Contexts

Upstate New York is an interesting mix of urban and rural space: busy streets running alongside of shopping malls; desolate roads running alongside the Great Lakes. The diversity of its geography parallels the diversity of its people. To the untrained eye, however, the diversity might be missed or simply assumed, just as the people who live here often take for granted the contrasts between the concrete streets of its cities and the barren slopes of its lake bluffs. And yet, it is there.

The diversity of the cities is outwardly talked about—the diversity of the rural areas is hidden, silenced, except for the occasional newspaper story (a letter to the editor that chronicles the fight of migrant workers to be allowed to have drinking water or access to toilets in the fields, for example, taking headlines and large blocks of time on the local television news programs). The news is always dismal. In an area rich with technological, health care, service, and agricultural resources, those who live in the most central and most peripheral areas of the region are denied the opportunities these abundant and lucrative jobs have to offer. In a city that boasts one of the largest amounts of Ph.D.s per capita in the country to the farms that maintain New York State's agriculture industry as its largest, the percentage of high school graduates among the general populace remains strikingly low (New York State Department of Education, 1995). This percentage is at its highest among those of color, who are poor and speak another language as their first language.

I was raised in upstate New York (having returned there after spending 5 years in New York and 15 years in Chicago) and so was intimately aware of the contrasts and of the missed opportunities that many of its people lived with on a daily basis. One of my first impressions upon my return to the area seemed familiar, in fact, in Proust's terms, the familiarity was there because I could feel it, I could taste it; and so it was mine:

> the student teacher continued her lesson as I gazed out the window of an elementary classroom to the city below, and there, as I had remembered in times past, casting its huge paternal shadow over the school in which teachers brought their own toilet tissue, was the Eastman Kodak Company. (Fieldnotes, student teacher observation, 2/95)

As I now reflect on this striking image, and others, often curious, from my childhood, the irony becomes almost unbearable, and I can feel it. Just who is operating from a culture of refusal? Just who is denying the existence of whom? And why?

Gaining access to work with an adolescent population that lived and went to school within that shadow was an interesting task. It was a task full of contradictions and ironies. Most people did not even know that these groups existed, and if they did, they certainly were not interested in working with them. In fact, from the very first day in which I began to make inquiries, I was met with curious looks and a multitude of questions.

"Just why would you want to go there?" one of my colleagues asked me, when I announced to my department that I was looking into gaining access into some of the jail classrooms around the area. "God!" another one declared, "Leave it to you, Blake!" More curious, I thought, was the reaction to my desire to work with migrant workers' children (and even to place student teachers among them), bolstered by the question, again from a colleague, "But, where *do* they live?" Indeed, I thought, there must be a whole group of adolescents that even the teacher educators I worked with couldn't be bothered with—a group of adolescents whose culture of refusal must be most profound.

Migrant Adolescents

They hit the fields by dawn and spend 12 to 14 hours inching their way through dirt hot as beach sand. Weed now, harvest later. The job doesn't change from year to year, and neither for that matter, does the life. (Nieves, 1996, B1)

Colleen's friend diligently stops the van at the stop sign. I turn my head both ways and for a moment I wonder why she bothers to stop; we are so far out in the country all I can see is fields: no houses, no cars, no people. Colleen, an ESL teacher, continues to talk to me, describing in quick sentences the conditions of the migrant camp I am about to visit for the first time. "It's better that we have [my] children with us, that way we're less of a threat and no one will run." "Yesterday," he continues, "the border patrol raided the camp with their sirens roaring and guns pulled." Colleen has helped create a frightening image in my mind: young children barefooted and staring, mothers and fathers confused and exhausted, being "ticketed" and told, in English, that they must leave the country by a certain date.

The camp, indeed, is a frightening place to a first–time visitor like myself; co–mingled with the smell of garbage that has carefully been placed in black bags in a bin, overflowing, not having been picked up in weeks, is the acid–chemical smell of the porta–potties, perhaps, too, overflowing, not having been emptied for the same amount of time. And yet, the camp seems also a warm place: a place that also smells of food cooking; a place that, today, abounds with sounds of laughter and music and of children playing as mothers and fathers return from 14–hour–long days in the fields to their "homes"—cinder block barracks with a communal kitchen area, ready to share the evening meal. Colleen finds the child she has come to see, and speaking in Spanish asks him to please come back to summer school. He smiles, they talk some more, she gives him a bag of clothes, pats him on the shoulder, and we leave. We begin the long drive back in silence; I don't even notice the stop sign this time, my head remains low and bowed; somehow the ritual of glancing side–to–side has become far less important.

By definition, migrant workers are those adults "who travel 75 or more miles in search of crop work" (Martin, Gordon, Kupersmidt, 1995, p.276). The Immigration Reform and Control Act on agriculture reports, based on this definition, that there are approximately "840,000 migrant farm workers [within the United States] who have 409,000 children traveling with them as they [seek out and] do farm work." Ninety–four of migrant farm workers are Latino and, therefore, speak Spanish as their first language (Martin, et al., 1995, p.276).

Migrant workers' numbers are estimated to be roughly between 25,000 and 75,000 throughout New York State with the most heavy concentration of workers in upstate New York (Nieves, 1996, B1). They are considered the "backbone" of the farming and agricultural industry of New York State, the State's number–one industry.

No significant research, however, has been written on migrant workers' children, who, as school–age children, are permitted by law to attend school for as long as their families are working in a particular district as farm workers. In other words, the workers and their children who are most vital to New York State's number–one industry, are among the most understudied, and therefore, the most invisible and silenced members of the state's "minority," second–language population.

Incarcerated Youth

Most prisons today offer fewer chances to positively influence the course of someone's life. Most "correctional" facilities have little or nothing to do with correcting. The resultant punitive environment makes a clear statement: Rehabilitation is not the system's goal. "Frills" like learning to read…are steadily being eliminated (Upchurch, 1996, p. 215).

The voice on the other end of the phone was angry and defensive. "Why do you want to observe my students?" she asked, adding, "They don't do much of anything here, there's just no learning going on." As I tried to explain who I was and why I would like to come in to visit, observe, and talk to the youth in her GED classes, she interrupted me many times, seemingly frustrated and exasperated at my inability to understand how "bad" it was "in here." "We have lots of race problems here, this is not the wealthy suburbs, you know," inferring, I thought, that I was a wealthy suburbanite (I am not) who just wanted to gaze upon the less fortunate, the "Other." "Yes, I know," I replied, "I've worked in urban schools for many years and just am curious to know how these students might be alike or different," stumbling for words to try to justify what was becoming clear to me as "Othering", doing just what she was accusing me of. Her voice rose to a high pitch and she screamed at me, "I thought this was about cultural diversity!" as she then, loudly, hung up the phone in my ear.

I was stunned. I had been asked to call the teachers at the jail as the "final" step in the research proposal process I had been conducting for months to visit classrooms in prisons around the area. I had already secured formal written permission by the city school district (they provide the teachers) and oral permission from the Major, who is in charge of daily operations for this particular facility. Access had been extremely tough, and I did not want it "ruined" now by a teacher whom I thought at the time, had simply burned out.

Much research has been written on the prison population in general (e.g., funding, new sites for building, changing population, public awareness and opinion (Firestone, 2001, pp. A1, A10) and a significant, yet small, body of literature has been written on the positive correlation between youth school dropout rates and incidence of incarceration (Ayers, 1997; Fine, 1994). Little, however, has been written to describe the potential magnitude of this correlation and its connection to and the significance of the out–of–school learning experiences of these youth.

This is a crucial area for educational research, particularly for youth of color. In 1995, one out of every three black men between the ages of 18 and 30 were either incarcerated or caught up in the criminal justice system in some way. The homicide rate for black youth ages 15 to 24 was seven to eight times higher than that of white youth of comparable ages. Early in the 21st century, it is predicted, two–thirds of the United States prison populations will be people of color, with the adolescent population showing the most growth. More adolescents of color in jails, of course, translates into fewer adolescents of color in schools.

Upstate New York reflects a higher trend for incarcerated minority youth, in general, than the rest of the nation, although recent media reports put the homicide rate at its lowest total since 1990 (Hand, 1999, pp. 1A, 8A). This represents a 23% drop since 1990 and a reverse in a trend, most touted by 1997 statistics, that showed upstate New York with an enormous increase in homicides, defying national decreases in homicide rates overall.

The same report credits this lowering trend to law enforcement's "closer attention to low–level drug dealing and gun trafficking and a new system for tracking statistics," (Hand, 1999, p. 8A) as well as a drastic increase in the arrest rate for low level drug sales and possession—almost five times as high as in 1997. These "low–level" criminals were the students in the jail classrooms in which I observed, their numbers swelling from 10 to over 25 (in each class) by the time I had stopped formally working with the students.

The ironies and injustices of the reality of these statistics are virtually lost in the media's reports, however. Why is it, we need to ask, are we incarcerating men and women from oppressed racial groups at unprecedented rates? Why, if the crime rate has fallen, are incarceration rates growing? (This was particularly obvious in upstate New York as monies were constantly being approved to upgrade and even build new facilities to ease the overcrowding.) Why, given that, as Fine & Weis (1998) point out, "national surveys indicate equal levels of drug use for Whites" that Blacks still make up the greatest proportion of inmates? Why, as Ayers (1997) states that only 6% of all juvenile crime is considered to be "serious and violent" are incidents of juvenile incarceration on the rise? How can we as a society justify locking up entire groups of adolescents—children in many senses—without understanding the "crushing power of poverty and social isolation" (Ayers, 1997, p. 41) that most of them have lived with on a daily basis?

These adolescents are meant to be locked away. Like their migrant counterparts, they are unseen and unheard, and therefore are less likely to be a threat—to themselves, and certainly to all of us. Their hidden status became excruciatingly clear to me as I tried to gain access to their lives and literacies outside of school.

Access, Representation, and Data Analysis

Gaining access to these adolescents both physically and emotionally was an exercise in learning to understand the sheer might of debilitating and punitive institutions like migrant camps and jails. These adolescents are hidden away for a reason, and as a result are literally carefully guarded from the rest of society. The migrants were not behind physical bars, but their cinder block homes were so far out in the country, surrounded in the hot summer months by fields and fields of tall cornstalks, that no one would need discover, nor mingle, with them, anyway. The adolescents in the jails were, of course, physically behind bars, kept away from "good" citizens like myself not only by guns and nightsticks, but also by the system itself. Outsiders were not welcome; I always felt the looks of suspicion from the law enforcement personnel, just as I heard the sounds of resentment from farmers who questioned why I would want to work with "those lazy migrants." And yet, I did get in, first at the migrant summer school program, then a migrant camp, followed by "social" chats with some of the influential farmers in the area, and finally equipped with my own security pass, into the jail classrooms and the residential "blocks" of various inmates as well as the working spaces of some law enforcement personnel.

Studying Down/Studying the Other

Jaffee (1993) claims that we are never altogether different from others, so that theoretically, for example, we are never, "wholly `Other'" from those we are studying. And yet these adolescents and I were different in very crucial ways, as our races, linguistic backgrounds, and social statuses worked to define and separate us wholly and totally from one another.

These socio–cultural notions of who we were had been firmly entrenched in all levels of society, historically constructed by collective perceptions, perspectives, and even expectations of who each one of us was. These created constructs forced us to maintain a distance from one another—to necessitate that I stand on the outside gazing inward—further exacerbated by the fact that these adolescents knew themselves to be the Other, a notion that was reinforced daily, often brutally, on them via the media and the physical and emotional boundaries built to keep them separate from the rest of society.

At the same time, though, it became apparent that through our struggles and explorations, we were actually making less problematic our differing statuses, particularly as I began to make *myself* more problematic. Fine (1994) describes this as "a necessary struggle" that involves attempts to "reconcile the slippery constructions of self and Other" and render, then, those created constructions "fluid" rather than "fixed" (p. 78). In other words, however different and distant, the self and the Other are always "knottily entangled." Confronting this entanglement as a major prerequisite for honest representation, then, has not only provided the kind of rich context the adolescents would choose to be seen in, but also the sorts of profound contradictions that we all knew existed in any social or political enterprise. Herein, though, lies the cruelty of the

profound contradictions: representing the Other *honestly* from a privileged, and historically, *dishonest* position.

Frankenberg (1993) claims that racism is not "merely an option for white people [as it] shapes white people's lives and identities in a way that is inseparable..." (p. 6). According to Frankenberg (1993), then, we must name our whiteness as we acknowledge that under and within all circumstances our whiteness "still confers race privilege [as an] economic and political category...avowedly historically specific and politically engaged" (p. 12). Only then, when this acknowledgment is made, can "racial dominance and whiteness emerge as complex, lived experiences..." (p. 21) that can be represented and "analyzed."

And yet Fordham (1996, personal communication) claims that studying the Other is a profound contradiction in itself. In fact, she considers studying the Other to be "studying down," and calls it, in no uncertain terms, a "cowardly act." Because it is easy to study those who are weak and powerless, she says, we minimize our guilt by trying to "chronicle their lives" in ways in which we see fit; we act as what Walkerdine (in Alvermann, 1992) has described as the "surveillant others" in committing what Alvermann (1992) calls the "voyeuristic" acts of research (p. 1). The profound contradictions, then, become, according to Fordham, the precise mechanisms by which we do nothing; we transform nothing. Instead, she admonishes, we need to, represent the struggle by "studying up," by studying the practices and policies of the institutions that force these adolescents, for example, to be so powerless.

The critical issue may lie in our abilities to question *ourselves* as we explore the political and ethical frameworks from which we conduct our work and represent others' voices. I believe we must address and confront the profound contradictions in our work as we, at the same time, acknowledge that this work is highly political and contentious. Like Fine (1994), I believe we must understand that tensions between the self and the Other are never "resolved in the neutral or by not getting involved" (p. 76), so that we must "exuberantly" put the struggle back into our texts, *at all levels*, so that we can truly work toward honest representation. The adolescents here have been represented in what I hope is their own terms. Like Ayers (1997), I have "scrambled physical descriptions,...compressed time and...invented names [so as to alter] revealing details of their lives" (xi), and yet I have left their voices intact. Passions, dreams, hopes, disappointments, anger, and even violence, will render itself real, sometimes raw, through these pages, but the kids' names and identities still will remain unidentifiable.

In this book, I attempt to represent the broader picture, too, talking with and representing in various ways throughout this text, those whom Fordham would consider to be in power: myself, teachers, administrators, officers, social workers, farmers, case managers, tutors and guards. Like the adolescents with whom I worked, my portrayals of myself and the others are, perhaps, full of contradictions, but in most cases, too, full of hope. Whether or not I indeed "got it right" will be left up to the many, and varied, interpretations of the many and varied people represented here.

Data Analysis

Like Rogers (1993), I have not set out to "test hypotheses about human development" (p. 269), so that certain theoretical constructs do not, and cannot, reveal and reflect that which I attempted to capture through my observations with the adolescents. As in my previous work, Blake (1997), and that of Brown & Gilligan (1992), Rogers (1993), and others, I, in anticipating analyzing my data, had to build into my design the space for these adolescents to speak in their own voices. That is, I had to relinquish the idea of a clearly–delineated analysis schema for one which, perhaps messy and unpredictable, more accurately and honestly reflected the youth's voices through their stories.

Here, the data analysis can best be described as a process of "productive ambiguity"(Eisner, 1997) as the preparations for and the processes of analysis were "suspended or at least subordinated to the processes of listening" (Andersen & Jack, 1991, p. 15) with the hope that the resultant data, on face value, is "more evocative than denotative, and in its evocation,...generates insight and invites attention to complexity" (p. 8).

In this book, I have welcomed the notion of "productive ambiguity" in attempting to describe, to explore, and perhaps to "analyze" these kids' lives and literacies with them. I hope that through their own words, my descriptions and representations of them can be read and understood for what they are, resulting, perhaps, in "less closure [but] more plausible interpretations of the meaning of the situation" (p. 8).

This work, still, is only one representation of the many voices that need to be heard. And yet, like my study among adolescent girls in Chicago (Blake, 1997), if one teacher finds a point of connection among my words to her students, then my attempt at representing these kids has been worth the effort. It is after all a work "undertaken with faith":

> faith in the mysterious depth and infinite complexity of life as it is lived, commitment to an enduring expectation that people can be better. It is tempered by the certainty that every attempt to convey a life is partial and contingent. It may extend the natural history of children in schools, it may enlarge our understandings of choice
>
> and language and writing, but it is not the last word. It may be an important antidote to authoritarian research and empty promises. It can contribute more details, more instances, more cases. Still, there is always more to say. This is one utterance (Ayers, in Blake, 1997, xiii).

Chapter Three

Theoretical Review: Adolescent Culture and the Culture of Refusal

In the best of circumstances, the tasks and strivings of adolescence are tumultuous...purposelessness and rolelessness creates a heightened sense of despair and an increased risk of disaster. Add to this the devastating effects of poverty, violence, and drugs, and the passage of adolescence becomes absolutely treacherous (Ayers, 1997, p. 140).

The onset of adolescence is a critical period of biological and psychological change for every child involving dramatic transitions in one's physical as well as one's social environment. These "transitions" have become more difficult in recent years as a combination of socio–economic factors has led to an "erosion" of the traditional social–support networks (schools, family, and community) upon which adolescents so desperately depend. And yet, little, if any, work done on adolescence prior to the 1980s has focused on the implications of the loss of these support systems. And, further, little, if any, work since the 1980's has taken into account the dramatic effects that gender, race, and class have on adolescence, nor has any examined these intersections within the context of such a rapidly changing, and increasingly violent, social environment. Simply put, we know far too little about the relationship between adolescence, ethnic identity, and the perceptions and expectations of multiply–marginalized youth, the youth Ayers (1997) so eloquently describes as having a "treacherous" ride into adulthood.

In this chapter, I will first historically situate commonly–held theories on adolescence and individual development, beginning with Freud (1978) Erikson (1963, 1968) and Kohlberg (1981, 1987) and moving on to Gilligan (1982, 1990) and the "new literature" on boys (Faludi, 1999; Garbarino, 1999; Pollack, 1998; Real, 1997). I will then examine some of the cultural and social factors at play in adolescents' lives, emphasizing the roles of family and community as crucial contexts in which adolescents develop. With this in mind, I will examine recent literature that points toward the "staggering array of guises" (Strauss, p.vii) that violence takes among adolescents, and the importance of recognizing that violence, too, can best be understood by placing it in socio/cultural and historical contexts. And finally, I will turn toward a discussion of the notion of "adolescence as social policy" as I explore the role of the school, examining, in particular, how and why multiply–marginalized youth share "precious little with other [adolescent] groups" (Strauss, p. 4). Exacerbated by institutionalized racism and fueled by the reality of the poverty and the lack of opportunity within the outside community, school simply becomes another place where these adolescents experience loss, precipitously entering a "culture of refusal".

Historical Settings: Individual Development

At the turn of the 20th century, adolescence was believed to be a time of "ambiguous and prolonged transition" (Straus, p. 4) in part because of an intense interplay between sexual and moral life (Freud, 1978) that needed to be resolved. In fact, this dichotomous notion of adolescence as a time period in which sexuality interrupted one's moral reasoning and thereby one's subsequent successful transition into adulthood remained firmly entrenched in the work of psychologists well into the 1980s, and still can be found today in selected pieces of research on the topic.

Kaplan (1984), for example, centered much of her discussion on the physical manifestations of adolescence, including, most notably, work on the harmful effects of masturbation. If unchecked, she claimed, adolescent masturbation would "serve regression and impede the forward–moving aspects of adolescent development" (p. 201) as well as "threaten[ing] the needs of the larger social community" (p. 196).

At the same time, researchers were re–visiting the notion of "turmoil theory" to explain the rite of passage of adolescents. Led by Erikson (1963, 1968), turmoil theory, re–coined as "identity crisis theory," posited that adolescents were not able to function well until they encountered a series of struggles that would help them form their own identities. The primary task of the adolescent, therefore, was to develop an "ego identity," as he or she struggled with developing "basic" skills that included literacy, intimacy, and problem solving. This was predicated, however, on the premise that adolescents had an overall sense of "personal safety." If adolescents were unable to develop this sense of self within a safety network, they then would fall prey to "role confusion", and become dangerously vulnerable to "delinquency, peer pressure, and…severe psychological disturbances" (Straus, 1994, p. 3). Erikson, importantly, too, was one of the first researchers to link personal identity and its evolution with the changing nature of culture and social change. Kohlberg (1981, 1987), on the other hand, reframed Freud's original work on the connections between identity development and moral development. Essentially, Kohlberg claimed that in order for adolescents to develop any sense of personal identity, thereby gaining entrance into adulthood, they needed to adopt a common understanding of a *"singular"* notion of morality.

Based on a longitudinal study of 84 boys (almost all white and middle class) over a period of 20 years, Kohlberg (1981) developed a model of "normal" cognitive development that included an acceptance of a code in which "moral dilemmas are discussed and resolved in a manner which will stimulate moral behavior" (p. 675), i.e., an "ethic of justice." Because young women (and presumably young men who were not middle class and white) did not see right and wrong in the same way as young men in the study did (i.e., they did not always hold an "ethic of justice" as central to a notion of morality and moral behavior), they experienced an abnormal transition into adulthood. Young women (and young men) who did not articulate an ethic of justice, therefore, were presumed to have critical gaps in their abilities to conduct moral reasoning and exhibit moral behavior.

In her crucial work of the 1980s, however, Gilligan (1982) presented an alternative theory of adolescent development that examined, specifically, a *female* model of transition. In this model, "morality is conceived in interpersonal terms and goodness is equated with helping and pleasing others" (p. 18). Grounded in opposition to the "ethic of justice" that served the white, male privilege so well, this "ethic of care" firmly re–centered young women's (and others') cognitive and moral development within a stable, balanced, and thereby "normal" framework. Gilligan's work, for the first time, had begun to shift the understandings of adolescent transitions to include more perspectives and voices. Interestingly, although Erikson (1963, 1968) had attempted to make connections between his theories of identity development to the changing nature of society, it was not until Gilligan's work that any notion of discussion of identity development was discussed outside of the "normal white male" range.

Adolescent Girls and a Loss of Voice

According to Gilligan (1990), it is absolutely crucial at the early adolescent stage (usually considered to begin around the fifth grade or at 10 years of age) for girls not to separate formal education from other powerful out–of–school learning experiences. As young women learn to deal with evolving emotional issues such as connection and relationship, and learn to deal with the perceived validity of these evolving emotions, they require guidance, role models, and confirmation to further their emotional development. Instead, however, because formal education has traditionally centered on other issues—i.e., autonomy, independence, detachment, and separation, adolescent girls not only begin to "observe where and when women speak and when they are silent" (Gilligan, 1990, p. 25), but also begin to learn precisely how to separate formal educational experiences from their other learning experiences. In other words, girls learn, and internalize, that what they consider to be central to their learning and knowledge lies, in fact, outside of any formal school realm. Girls understand that the image of the nice girl is so persuasive that they learn to modulate, silence, or appropriate others' voices altogether.

Feminist researchers (Belenky et al., 1986; Fine 1987, 1991a; Gilligan, 1982, 1990; Gilbert, 1989, 1991) see an appropriation of voice as extremely problematic for girls. Because girls have traditionally held few positions from which to speak (Gilbert, 1989), they typically learn to do what these researchers have called "doubling" their voices. This doubling of voice is considered to be a direct response to a situation of a "deeply–knotted dilemma of being at once inside and outside of the world they are entering as young women" (Gilligan, 1982, p. 148). In other words, girls feel they must present separate voices depending on the context, audience, purpose, and theme for both speaking and writing.

Fine's (1987) work among urban adolescent girls supports the notion that girls learn to develop two or more separate voices. "Good" girls trained themselves to speak and produce in two voices, one academic, and one at the margin. While the academic voice was one that denied class, gender, and race and "reproduced ideologies about hard work, success, and their "natural" sequence; and stifled the desire to disrupt" (p. 163), the marginal voice expressed more private experiences and struggles such as those that *revolved around* discussions of gender, race, and class. This particular two–voice dilemma was often more permanently resolved by "creative, if ultimately self–defeating strategies" (p. 164) such as dropping out of school.

One major result of this emphasis on the differing experiences of girls' transitions into adulthood has been to re–examine boys' development, finally, perhaps, from within the socio–cultural perspective so desperately lacking in any early studies.

The New Literature on Boys: A Loss of Heart

Recently, both psychologists and educators (Faludi, 1999; Gilligan, 1982; Garbarino, 1999; Pollack, 1998; Real, 1997) have begun to write that "a national crisis of boyhood" (Hall, 1999, p. 33) is upon us. Tragically realized before much of the research reached the mainstream public (see news accounts on the school shootings by adolescent males in Littleton, Jonesboro, Springfield, and Columbine High School in Colorado, 1998 and 1999), the crisis has now captured the attention of the general public. In a desperate attempt to ascribe blame, however, policy and lawmakers seem to have obscured (or discounted) the very real challenges inherent in the volatile social environment that adolescents are faced with at the beginning of the 21st century. And yet, as a result of the school tragedies (and partly fueled by the AIDS epidemic), a new "masculine ideology" (Pleck, 1988) has emerged from the literature. Called the "new literature" on boys, this ideology measures risk for dangerous sexual behavior, substance use, educational problems, and encounters with law enforcement and the criminal justice system by the degree to which males subscribe to traditional roles (e.g., a need for physical toughness; a reluctance to talk about problems; an unwillingness to do things "feminine," such as housework or childrearing; and an undying need for respect of masculinity). That is, boys who have difficulty reconciling the traditional values of their fathers and other older male relatives with a feminist culture that celebrates sensitivity and girls' voices are in danger of becoming "undone."

According to Real (1997), for most boys, becoming a man is not so much an acquisition of something good, but a disavowal of something bad. He explains:

> When researchers asked girls and women to define what it means to be feminine, the girls answered with positive language: to be compassionate, to be connected, to care about others. Boys and men, on the other hand, when asked to describe masculinity, predominantly responded with double negatives. Boys and men did not talk about being strong so much as about not being weak. They do not list independence so much as not being dependent. They did not speak about being close to their fathers so much as about pulling away from their mothers. In short, be[coming] a man generally means not being a woman. As a result, boys' acquisition of malehood is a negative achievement...Masculine identity development turns out to be not a process of development at all but rather a process of elimination, a successive unfolding of loss. (p. 130)

This successive unfolding is undoubtedly exacerbated by the effects of race and class. In an adolescent world already fraught with strife and confusion, multiply–marginalized adolescent males, in particular, attempt to make the transition into adulthood amidst social systems designed to segregate and punish, rather than include and support.

Cultural and Social Settings: Family and Community Roles

The family remains the primary group from which adolescents learn the norms and social expectations of human behavior, as well as the most important source from which children receive emotional nurturance. In fact, much like the developmental research on the individual, family life–cycle theories address the various stages that adolescents must complete from within the familial structure itself, a structure that, once again, must be perceived as "safe." And yet, family life–cycle theories become distinct from individualistic theories in that here the development, that is the emotional and economic stability of the family, directly impacts adolescents' growth.

Today, one in four adolescents is raised in a single–parent household where 70% of the mothers in those households are working and 46% of those households are poor, with a median income of only $9,000. Adolescents are greatly over–represented among poverty populations of all races, but among Blacks that figure mirrors the general populace at 46.1%; among Latinos it is slightly lower, at 40.9%. (As a single parent of a 15–year–old son who, along with family and friends, has raised him exclusively since he was two years old, I cringe when I hear that "single mothers" are to blame for societal ills, and I, therefore, in no way mean to imply that children cannot be "successful" in single parent households.) Further, there is a strong positive correlation between poverty i.e., economic stability, and parental availability and support i.e., emotional stability, and "delinquency" and violence. Children raised in poverty, with parents who are either working long or unusual hours or who have become too isolated and disenfranchised to care for children on a level that white mainstream society sees fit, often find that they have little to depend on both emotionally and financially within their homes. Lacking resources and the ability to tap into the support systems available to other adolescents, poor adolescents often react to the victimization they endure by engaging in "anti–social" or violent behavior. (A caveat here, too: obviously there are other important factors at work besides poverty as evidenced, again, by the school shootings in white middle–class and upper–middle–class communities.)

Fifty thousand adolescents—a number equivalent to all of those Americans who died in the Vietnam War—have been killed in violent acts in the United States since 1979 (Strauss, 1994, p. xiv). Although typically violence flourishes where familial abuse, neglect, poverty and societal and institutional racism and inequities abound, putting urban, poor adolescents most at risk, recent research (Dryfoos, 1990) claims that violence in the 2000s will cut across social and economic lines. A staggering one in four adolescents today will experience a form of violence so severe, that they "have little chance of becoming responsible adults." In fact, Dryfoos (1990) sees the problem so overwhelming that she states:

> a new class of untouchables is emerging in our inner cities, on the social fringes of suburbia, and in some rural areas: young people who are functionally illiterate, disconnected from school, depressed, prone to drug abuse and early criminal activity, and eventually, parents of unplanned and unwanted babies (p. 3).

Violence in adolescence is primarily the result of the profound economic, social, and political inequities that many adolescents are faced with on a daily basis. In a society dominated and controlled by an entrenched patriarchy, poor adolescents, in particular, find few adults whom they can look up to and on whom they can model their behavior. Violence, therefore, becomes an adaptive, and often a sole, coping mechanism.

Adolescence as Social Policy: School, Cultural Compatibility Theory and a Culture of Refusal

The violence so prevalent in our communities today makes it an unrealistic expectation that schools alone can prepare adolescents for work, further education, and life in general. The debilitating living conditions that so many of our youth encounter as routine make it a difficult task indeed for these adolescents to succeed in a traditional school setting. Incongruent with their life experiences and unprepared to give the support these adolescents so desperately need, middle or junior high schools typically become the very sites where delinquency develops.

At the turn of the 20th century it was thought that all adolescents' lives and experiences were incongruent with the way schools had been set up and run. Therefore, it was decided that schooling for adolescents needed to be re-conceptualized, and thus, the idea of the junior high school was born. Essentially, the junior high school was established to differentiate, and isolate, as well as to help society create a means and a context in which to not only "protect" but also to help "sort" adolescents for future work and careers. At the same time, three major social policy changes were being enacted to coincide with the invention of the junior high school. These were mandatory high school, the juvenile justice system (see Ayers' 1997 account), and federal legislation against child labor (Strauss, 1994, p. xi). These social policies, coupled with a new vision for the schooling of this age group, established "adolescence" as a bona fide developmental period between childhood and adulthood over which the government had much control. Out of policy makers' favor from the 1930s to the 1960s, junior high schools enjoyed a revival that eventually led to the modern–day creation of middle schools, the places where, it was believed, both the educational and developmental needs of adolescents could truly be met (Hechinger, 1993).

Today's middle schools, however, are still ill–defined. Seen as places where the transition could be eased from childhood to adulthood (and from elementary school to high school), where the notion of incongruence could be addressed and soothed, a lack of understanding (by teachers, administrators, and other support personnel, including parents) of what constitutes this transition is apparent. In fact, the middle school has been described as the "breeding ground for behaviors and attitudes that cause many students to drop out of school" (Takanishi, 1993, p. 73).

Realistically, though, we still know far too little about how these "incongruent" worlds "combine in the day–to–day lives of adolescents to affect their engagement in educational settings" (Phelan, Davidson,& Yu, 1998, p. 3). If we, for example, believe, as Giroux (In Jipson et al., 1995, x) would have us believe, that "schools function as cultural sites actively engaged in the production of not only knowledge but also social identities," then we might come to understand how poor youth, in particular, seek to develop their social identities outside of school, where cultural space and expectations of everyday life are in line with their daily experiences.

Cultural compatibility theory seeks to describe and explain this incongruence and lack of common cultural space between minority youths' lives and experiences at home and their lives and experiences in school. Cultural compatibility theory research not only draws on observational data to document the important differences between home and school for minority youth, but also describes in detail the rich, though different, home and school learning environments within which these students live and learn. Much of what we have learned from cultural compatibility theory has provided us with empirical evidence that supports the claim that "problematic" interactions in schools [among minority youth] are, in fact, related to cultural differences (Heath, 1983; Trueba, Guthrie, & Au, 1981; Trueba & Delgado–Gaitan, 1988).

The notion of cultural differences as a major factor in the challenge of the poor, urban adolescent's development is found in recent research that strongly posits that school is simply not "enveloping" enough to help these (and similar) adolescents approximate success. In a work entitled "Schools are not the answer," Traub (2000) argues that "school...as we understand it now, is not as powerful an institution as it seems." In effect, poor (urban) students' educational inequality, he claims, is not rooted in the school; rather, it is deeply entrenched in the existing social, cultural, and economic problems and challenges of the urban community. Coleman (in Traub,

2000) elaborates:

> the inequalities imposed on children by their home, neighborhood and peer
> environment are carried along to become the inequalities with which they con-
> front adult life at the end of school. (p. 55)

Coleman continues by saying that it is an "impossibility" to expect that
school can provide all of what he calls the "child's human and social capital," terms invented by social scientists in the 1960s to "describe and quan-
tify" the effects of family, community, and school on the developing child.
Human capital refers to all human capabilities that are passed along from
family to their children, accumulating like other capital, and "produced,"
in part by school. Social capital is defined as "the norms, the social networks, the relationships between adults and children that are of value for
the children..." (Coleman in Traub, 2000). Because of the enormous influence of the human and social capitals, "the effects of home and community
blotted out (emphasis mine) almost all those of school" (p. 57). The imbalance, therefore, once seen as being firmly entrenched in the lack of connections between home and school, is now regarded as being situated on
much larger continua. Where schooling, the resources of the local community, and the needs of the larger society in today's global, technological
workplace become at odds—where the school is not providing the extra
support missing from the family, the community is not providing the extra
support missing from both the family and the school, and the larger society
offers no support in the form of work—multiply–marginalized adolescents, in particular, become effectively engulfed in the *incongruence* of
their lives. This incongruence leads, then, precipitously to a culture of refusal, where it is believed that the lack of support systems are unnecessary,
unwanted, and certainly undermining of adolescents' true needs and de-
sires.

Adolescence was invented for specific reasons at a particular point in
history; its roots, therefore, are both social and political, and so, too, especially is the hopelessness, joblessness, and violence associated with it
(Straus, 1994, xiv). Contrary to the days where unskilled work could be
found in the industries of mass production, today's high–tech society requires finely–tuned skills, particularly in what the *New York Times* once
called "the manipulation of letters and symbols." Further, the obsolescence
of our traditional learning systems as well as a changing, global economy
that depends increasingly more on human resources has, in fact, most ad-
versely affected poor and minority students.

Undoubtedly, school remains a "pivotal institution" in adolescents'
lives. Along with the other major factors (e.g., family and community) that

strongly influence the adolescent's transition into adulthood, schools, too, remain notoriously ineffective in attending to "the social meanings of ethnicity and the identity development of minority adolescents" (Takanishi, 1993, p.56). Indeed, much of the current research states that "the real damage gets done in middle school" (Hall, 1999, p. 35). Being an adolescent in this society is intrinsically stressful, but among multiply–marginalized adolescents, the transitions into adulthood may be particularly so as race, class, and gender intersect to produce different and more pronounced patterns of anxiety and challenge.

We have a great need for continuity in schools (i.e., curricular and developmental) and congruence among social institutions (i.e., families, communities and community organizations, and schools). In essence, to begin, we need to give students the "cultural space within dominant arenas" (Ferrell, 1997, p. 22) where, "among marginalized kids, battles over cultural space, are...more intense...[as the] creation and contestation of cultural space shapes expectations/experiences of everyday life." Without such spaces, I argue, schools, as one crucial support system needed for adolescent development, fails the adolescent.

In upcoming chapters, I will further contextualize some of the different meanings associated with the numerous challenges that these adolescents face, specifically in the social arena of the school. A major focus throughout this book, however, will be just that, framed by the questions: How can we systematically study the social meanings of ethnicity, and the identity development of minority adolescent, and as a result, how can social institutions become more attuned to adolescents? If marginalized adolescents are not getting congruency from the social institutions designed to offer that support, how can we help provide it?

Multiply–marginalized adolescents, just like all adolescents, are "avid seekers of moral authenticity" (Ayers, 1997, p. 139) and yet they come face–to–face with a society that disdains them, i.e., does not legitimize their understandings of themselves and their perspectives of their social world. Like the girls about whom Brown & Gilligan (1992) write, marginalized adolescents learn, too, to separate their formal education experiences—to refuse their formal educational experiences—for more powerful learning experiences in out–of–school contexts, taking their voices, their cultural spaces, and their literacies underground, to that place I call "a culture of refusal."

Chapter Four

Theoretical Review: Local Literacies

Literacy is at the heart of world development and human rights. Its importance lies in what precedes literacy: the words that are the expression of human thought...the written word allows infinite possibilities of transmission and therefore of active participation in communication. These possibilities are what make the goal of universal literacy so important (Mayor, 1999, xi).

Formal schooled literacy practices and the autonomous model on which they are based may indeed have facilitated power for some: but they will not necessarily provide power for many, when the kinds of literacy needed in their specific contexts are often very different and, in a social sense, more complex (Street, 2001, 13).

Why should I write? I have nothing to say. Writing is evil. (Fieldnotes, 6/96)

Say the word "literacy" among educators and you will have undoubtedly begun a debate; say the word "literacy" among migrant or incarcerated adolescents who have endured years of unsuccessful attempts at becoming literate in the traditional or "schooled" sense, and you will have opened a Pandora's box—a box where only evil lurks inside.

The debate among educators may sound something like this: Do we return to a "traditional" approach to teaching literacy where we employ techniques such as teacher–led grammar drills that focus on categories and names of the structures of language—a technical and neutral skill—or do we embrace "alternative" pedagogies that seek to engage students at all levels as they learn to construct and reconstruct language and literacy within the social world around them—a social and cultural engagement?

According to Gee (1996, p. 122), most educators (and hence most laypeople) still regard a traditional approach as the "master myth of literacy and language." From this perspective, language and literacy are regarded as commodities that can be "quantified and exchanged for economic mobility." Traditional literacy approaches still retain an aura of the "powerful" and a calling from the "almighty"; a calling that migrant adolescents, for example, feel they will never be able to answer with any measure of success.

In this chapter, I will review some of the historical understandings that have shaped our perceptions of what it means to be literate today in the United States and across the Western world. Next, I will introduce and describe the terms "schooled" and "local" literacies while situating these approaches along what Hornberger & Skilton–Sylvester (1998) call a "literacy continua" And finally, I will end with a discussion on Street's (2001) "ideological" approach to literacy, while reviewing current global perspectives on literacy, and literacy and social change.

A Checkered Past

Our beliefs about literacy and "good" literate practices stem from a long, albeit checkered history dating from the Middle Ages. As Blake and Blake (2002) describe:

In the Middle Ages, a "litteratus" was simply a person who could read Latin. The ability to write was not included in this definition because apparently literate people found it difficult to master the skill of using ink and quills to write on very scarce and precious parchment, a writing surface made from the skin of a sheep or goat. After 1300 A.D. a "litteratus" was a person with a minimal ability to read Latin, mainly because of the breakdown of learning during the Middle Ages. After the Reformation, with the spread of vernacular languages, literate persons became those who could both read and write in their native languages.

Although we don't find the term "literacy" in English until the end of the nineteenth century, the actual ideas of "literate" and "illiterate" date from the last half of the sixteenth century. The classical definition of "literacy" survived until at least 1740, the evidence of which is a quote from Lord Chesterfield, as cited in the *Oxford English Dictionary*, in which an "illiterate" is "ignorant of Greek and Latin." (p. 10)

Literacy skills were equated with privilege; the rich were educated and, as such, read and wrote not only in Greek and Latin, but in their native tongues as well.

At the turn of the 20th century in America, that mind–set remained clearly entrenched in society's belief system. The governmental point of view, perhaps, extended this elitism even further as it regarded the printed word as being associated closely with the power to "domesticate" exotic cultures and was seen, therefore, as most useful in describing the writing systems of these cultures, as well as to offer Bible translation to the people who had been thereby "civilized." (In America, think: Native American populations.) Any pedagogical application (in schools) of the written word was made available to only a few, elite and usually male, students.

The aim of well–intentioned linguists such as Bloomfield (who were also offering their theories on language and literacy learning at the turn of the 20th century) to create a "value–free" science of language and writing had been firmly replaced by one that, highly empiricist and xenophobic, held as its goal to provide "every person [with] a New Testament in his [sic] own language" (Rodby, 1992, p. 5). Interest in writing for the masses was only seen useful as far as it could accomplish this goal. By the mid–20th century, writing (read: literacy) was clearly seen as a "civilizing" tool. Indeed, centered within the theoretical framework of the new, modern branch of linguistics, structural linguistics, was the increasingly–accepted notion that literacy was an elitist practice (p. 7) that could (and should) be mastered only by those who could successfully practice and control sentence patterns to produce coherent texts. Chomsky's groundbreaking work (1957) was the notable exception in claiming that literacy (and its practices) was indeed connected with thought as well as speech. Chomsky questioned the longstanding empiricist view of language and literacy to hypothesize that "general features of grammatical structure [were] common to all languages [and] reflect certain fundamental properties of the human mind" (p. 14). In other words, no one language or writing system (hence, no one literacy) was, in theory, privileged over another; each was bona fide in its own right.

Chomsky's view of language and literacy did not, and has not, prevailed throughout the Western world. Rather, a traditional Western view (one that was limited to a few elite and used among non–Western peoples as a civilizing tool) of a technical and neutral set of skills has enjoyed primacy over non–Western traditions, particularly those where people relied on oral texts for communication and interaction. In fact, the Western perspective has been inextricably associated with social, political, and economic progress and those who ascribe to (and are thereby successful with) this "autonomous" form of literacy control those who are not. Street (2001) elaborates:

> [because] the meaning of a text and of literacy itself could be different, for example, for European colonists than it was for their subjects, [it] was the key to political control. (p. 94)

This "technical, rational" model still prevails throughout our schools today via literacy methodologies that focus on the technical features of language and discrete skills and remains, therefore, a tool that effectively forces all students (if they are to be successful) to accept a Western, literate ideology.

Interestingly, the academic research on literacy since the 1960s reflects this ideology and can be seen quite clearly in the plethora of work that has examined both the cognitive predictors (e.g., socio–economic class and parents' educational level and income) and the cognitive consequences (e.g., deprivation and correlation between literacy acquisition and dropout rates) of unsuccessful literacy and language development. Language difference, reflected most notably within the literacy practices of students whose predictors did not match white, so–called mainstream middle–class indicators, was recorded as "deficient," and remediation became the standard intervention to align students' literacy practices with the school's literacy practices. Students who did not acquire literacy in a traditional manner that reflected a standard, Western view were labeled, quite simply, "illiterate."

In the late 1970s and early 1980s, however, a grassroots movement of teachers began to flourish. Behind the closed doors of their classrooms, these teachers began implementing curricular and pedagogical change based on what they knew (observationally and intuitively) worked best in helping their students to become literate. The movement itself (alternately called "the whole language movement" (Blake, 1990, Goodman, 1986) and the "integrated language approach" (Pappas, 1990) was solidly grounded in reconstructed theoretical frameworks that afforded (i.e., gave permission to) teachers the opportunities to help students begin to take control of their own literacy learning and to move away from a technical view of literacy.

As a result of the whole language movement, both research and practice in holistic and process approaches was prolific throughout the 1980s (Atwell, 1987; Calkins, 1983, 1986; Goodman, 1986; Graves, 1983, 1986), showing quite clearly that students could and did become active participants in their own literacy learning, particularly in writing. Studies of successful classroom models of process writing, for example, highlighted how commonplace it was for students to become motivated to write more, to improve their grammar usage, and to develop a greater sense of community through writing at virtually every grade level. Further, the research on the efficacy of process approaches to literacy among "minority" and English–language learners (ELLs), although seemingly slower to develop, did emerge with notable studies highlighting success in general (Dyson & Freedman, 1990; Reyes, 1991) the importance of peer conferencing (Blake, 1992; Gere & Abbott, 1985) the ways in which research in native language literacy could be extrapolated to help explain acquiring literacy in a second language (Hudelson, 1989) and how ELLs, like their first language counterparts, when successful in moving back and forth among the processes of process writing, for example, could produce pieces exhibiting higher textual readability and coherence (Blake, 1992). Simply put, it was demonstrated that students from all walks of life (like the adolescents in jails and migrant camps I will describe here) had more access, and therefore more opportunity, to engage in and become successful in acquiring language and literacy skills.

And yet, as far as the process movement moved students' varied learning experiences, and the processes by which they engaged with these learning experiences, to the forefront of our common understanding of what it means to become literate, process approaches, too, fell short in acknowledging the multiple social, cultural, linguistic, and historical contexts in which students live, and from which they construct their literate selves.

In previous work (Blake, 1995,1997), I have attempted to extend the efficacy of process approaches to literacy, particularly as it pertained to a process approach to writing. Specifically, in this work, I advocated making explicit these multiple contexts from which urban, "minority" students in particular, practiced and appropriated literacy. Termed, "cultural texts," emphasis was placed on the

> intense social life past and present discourses have lived and have informed one's literacy practices. A cultural text smells of context (Blake, 1995, p. 397).

Among migrant or jailed adolescents, for example, then, it may evoke senses of gender, race, class, and/or aspirations, struggles, and realities that are different from the Western technical view.

From a "cultural text" perspective, then, an emphasis needs to be placed not only on how one's literacies are socially and culturally constructed from such notions as gender, race, and class, but on what these (re)–constructed literacies actually say, revealing crucial issues that are central to these adolescents' lives and literacies. However, even with an emphasis placed on gender, race, and class, for example, these holistic approaches to literacy are not necessarily "culturally validating" for all students simply because we intend them to be.

Willis (1995), with her own son's struggles with dominant literacy practices in school, asserts that:

> we need to understand where *he* acquired language and *his* understanding of culture, as well as *his* history of literacy instruction, to understand how *he* is "reading the world" of school literacy and how *his* experiences with a variety of school literacy forms, *including* holistic approaches, have *not* addressed his cultural ways of knowing, experiences, language, and voice (emphases mine) (p. 40).

Rather, as Willis (1995) explains, literacy does, "not evolve in one context or through one type of event; rather, it is a complex endeavor that is mediated through culture" (p. 40). Otherwise, she claims, school literacy becomes a "cultural accommodation" where students like her son "constantly make a mediating effort to help others understand events that appear to be commonplace on the surface, but are in fact culturally defined" (p. 32). As we shall see with the students I describe here, "refusal" replaces "cultural accommodation" as it appears commonplace to these students that *no one* will, in any event, understand.

Schooled Literacies versus Local Literacies

most of the conceptual advances in thinking about literacy in the last two decades have come from research on out–of–school literacy (Hull & Schultz, 2002, p. 2).

The "New Literacy Studies" of the late 1980s and 1990s that put forth the notion of a "plurality" of literacies was touted by researchers in the field as a reaction to the literacy crisis of the 1980s. Szwed (1981), a pioneer in the field of the New Literacy studies, claimed, in fact, that

despite the claims of a crisis of "illiteracy," we had not yet conceptualized literacy, nor did we know how literacy or reading and writing were used in social life (p. 14).

Szwed (1981) was one of the first researchers to look toward literacy in the community, away from the school, finding (among other things) that literacy was not a single entity, but rather that communities used "multiple" literacies to negotiate their places in the world. Today, researchers such as Heath (1983), Gee (1996), Street (2001), Willinsky (1990) focus on how this "plurality of literacies" is linked to power and power relations throughout the world.

Street's (1995) notion of local literacies reconceptualizes our previous work in holistic/process approaches, as it not only builds upon what we knew worked best, but extends the perspective of "literacy" to include a strong, ideological base. That is, literacy is an *ideological* practice that is embedded in the everyday social and cultural lives of people (their local literacies) and therefore reflects not a lack of traditional skills, but an addition—a complement to that which is most often taught in schools, and thereby "reified" by society and its government.

The reification of "schooled literacy" is in Street's view (1995, 2001) view done because schooled literacy is seen as something autonomous, universal, and neutral—a "gift" that a government or an educational system bestows upon people in order to lead them to "good social practices" (Street, 2001, p. 4). And schooled literacy, too, is seen as a civilizing factor—an equalizing factor that ameliorates the lack of social and economic opportunities that poor students would otherwise not have.

In classrooms, then, schooled literacy is realized through the teaching of Standard English (exclusively) and the use of a Western canon that not only directs (and/or mandates—see samples of state standards) literary choices, but literacy practices. Indeed, in Kell's (1997) words, schooled literacy can be defined as:

> sanctioned and thereby framed from within particular textual interpretative processes currently being canonized. (p. 242)

While the term "local literacies" has become a metaphor for agency and voice, schooled literacies remain in the realm of control and power.

The term local literacies represents an important ideological and conceptual shift in how the processes of reading and writing are viewed and interpreted, particularly in the schools. We need to reject the notion of an autonomous literacy as the only valid form of literacy and embrace the local literacies of the classroom. This, in turn, helps us to highlight and to emphasize the centrality of the social nature of literacy in reflecting the multiple ways in which context, culture, and material conditions affect specific literacy practices.

Local Literacies and a Continua of Literacy

Like Street (2001), Hornberger & Skilton–Sylvester (1998) believe that one literacy should not be rejected in lieu of another. (This becomes particularly crucial when talking about access to power and the opportunities to power that learning a schooled literacy affords. See Delpit, 1995, Street, 2001, and Willis, 1995,for extensive discussions of "minority" students being denied access to the language of power). In fact, Hornberger & Skilton-Sylvester posit that we should start from a less binary position where we view literacy and its practices upon a continuum, where, ideally, one can move across at will, choosing which literacy to use at which time. A continua of literacy is best described in terms of four frameworks that help define this infinite movement: context, development, content, and media. In Hornberger & Skilton–Sylvester's (1998) view, then, students' development of language and literacy should draw on all points of the continuum, not just those from the more or the less powerful ends.

Specifically, this continuum highlights quite clearly the distinct positions on the continuum that less powerful (i.e., local) and more powerful (i.e., schooled) literacies fall. In reality, because the more powerful end of the continuum contains points such as "monolingual," "written," "literary," "majority," "decontextualized," and "convergent scripts," becoming literate or biliterate in school and society clearly means focusing one's efforts almost exclusively on these aspects of language and literacy development. On the contrary, focusing on the other end of the continuum, where points such as "oral," "minority," "contextualized," and "divergent scripts" fall means that the act of becoming literate comes at a great risk. At this end, literacy development is relegated to the "personal," to the "oral," to the "expressive" and, therefore, is not deemed as appropriate in most school settings. While it would be advantageous for all literacy learners to be able to move along this continuum, in reality our schools do not allow this journey. The continuous emphasis on formal "schooled literacy" contexts gives support to the power and privilege schooled literacy enjoys at the expense of local literacies and the contexts in which these literacies are realized.

A Growing International Perspective

As schooled literacy practices are being increasingly canonized around the world (see various accounts on standards and reform in New York State, Bilingual Education Reform in California, Literacy Reform in South Africa, and National curriculum reform in the United Kingdom and the Czech Republic, for example), fueling a backlash toward alternative perspectives such as Hornberger & Skilton Sylvester's (1998), challenges are emerging from a body of international and critical literacy scholars whose work is based on theoretical frameworks based in socio–linguistics, ethnography and the ethnography of communication, and of course, the New Literacy Studies.

Led philosophically by Street (1995) and his work in South Africa, Iran, and the United Kingdom, Hornberger & Skilton–Sylvester (1998) in Cambodia, Puerto Rico, and among indigenous populations in the Andes mountains, and Kell (1997) in post–apartheid South Africa with her work among the settlement populations in Cape Town, these researchers have fashioned an ideological approach to literacy that, as a critical perspective, repositions entirely the notion of what it means to become literate. Rather than solely reflecting the outcomes of schooled literacy, their work emphasizes, quite simply yet eloquently, that throughout the world, literacy practices and behaviors are, regardless of the government or schools' efforts, in reality, grounded in the everyday lives and experiences of people in their homes and communities.

These scholars write about a crucial need for a synthesis of various notions and definitions of literacy (some of which I have discussed here). Specifically, for example, Street (1995, 2001) puts forth an ideological model that subsumes rather than excludes the work of the rational model; Hornberger & Skilton–Sylvester (1998) envision a continuum where literacy learners are encouraged to journey along all points; and Kell (1997) calls for those in power to understand literacy as a two–way process—a two–way process in which as those in power provide literacy access to those not in power, those in power learn, too, to "read...with [the] understanding of the discourses of those who have been marginalized" (p. 19).

Literacy and Social Change in the United States

While literacy and social change may go hand–in–hand in post-apartheid South Africa, for example, in the United States literacy is associated with the status quo. In fact, among the multiply–marginalized youth with whom I have worked, literacy works *against* their success. As they have endured years of racism in our schools while being told they do not have the abilities to become literate in today's technological society, the multiply–marginalized of the United States seem to have eschewed schooled literacy altogether. Fueled in part by a return to teaching and assessment of literacy attainment in discrete and decontextualized ways by states such as New York, which are tied to standards and accountability, advocating for "local literacies" as measures of success seems unlikely.

And yet, as social change in the United States seems a vestige of the past, a synthesis of national and international perspectives surrounding literacy and its relationship to economic, social, and political success seems a timely issue for the future. As the United States experiences another huge increase in immigrant populations (resulting in predictions that states such as California will house more non–native speakers of English than native speakers in the near future) the notion of what it means to become literate will be reshaped and perhaps redefined by these new majorities. And these literacies will indeed be shaped by the daily lives of these people in their homes and in their communities. An accepted synthesis of these literacies and those of the traditional, schooled realm would help us to better prepare our students for the "success" of the future.

Conclusion

In poor communities, in urban black communities or in rural Latino communities such as jail classrooms and migrant camps in the United States, much like the settlement communities of Cape Town in South Africa (Kell, personal communication, July 1997), for example, schooled literacy simply does not "articulate with the existing literacy practices in the community" and so, by its very nature, schooled literacy cannot (and does not, in and of itself) give voice or agency to those less powerful—to the multiply–marginalized youth of any poor urban and rural community. As a result, these youth either tune out or drop out, as they develop their own literacies and sets of discourses that reflect and represent their particular lives and experiences. Coupled with the challenging transitions into adolescence as described in Chapter 3, along with often crushing poverty, these students resist, reject, and ultimately deny both schooled literacy and school altogether, as they firmly place themselves within the culture of refusal.

Chapter Five

Fruit of the Devil:
The Migrant Summer School Program

Strawberries and cream. Strawberries dipped in chocolate. Strawberry short-cake, now that's a classic. The only problem with strawberries is somebody had to pick them. La fruta del diablo, that's what migrant workers call them. The fruit of the devil. Pick them long enough and they will break your back and mangle and stain your hands forever. (Reyes, 1995, p. 6B)

The conversation begins and ends the same way: "School sucks." "There's nothing here for me." Like picking strawberries, "schooled literacy" for the migrant workers' kids I worked with was indeed "the fruit of the devil," alternately seen as useless, boring, complicated, dangerous, and even "evil."

Evil? Yes! These migrant farm workers' adolescents had learned that what they had to say and to write about in school didn't count. They were constantly being censored or being told their work was "no good." "Why bother?" Angie, a 14–year–old Latina asked me. "I won't make no money doing this, and I can make sixty dollars a day in the fields!" (It is necessary that I add a note here: Most of the faculty and staff at the migrant project *summer school* they attended were very attentive to these students' needs, and most of the teachers there tried creatively, albeit desperately, to "undo" the students' perceptions.) As I discussed in the previous chapter, however, schooled literacy is a metaphor for issues of power, control, agency, and voice—the driving force behind characteristics that these students knew full well they neither possessed, nor had access to.

Who Are Migrant Workers?

By definition, migrant workers are those adults who travel 75 or more miles in search of crop work (Martin, 1994) and/or spend at least one–half of the year searching for and traveling to sites for employment. The Immigration Reform and Control Act on Agriculture reports, based on this definition, that there are approximately "840,000 migrant farm workers [within the United States] who have 409,000 children traveling with them as they [seek out and] do farm work." Ninety–four percent of migrant farm workers are Latino, and therefore, speak Spanish as their first language

(Martin, 1994). The average annual income of migrant fieldworkers is around $5,000.

Migrant workers' numbers are estimated to be roughly between 25,000 and 75,000 throughout New York State, with the heaviest concentration of workers in upstate New York (Nieves, 1996, p. B1). They are considered to be the "backbone" of the farming and agricultural industry of New York State, the state's number one industry. And yet, these workers and their children, vital to New York State's number–one industry, are the most understudied, invisible, and silenced members of the State's "minority," second–language population.

Who Are the Children of Migrant Workers?

According to New York State eligibility documents, a "migratory child" is a child whose parent, guardian, spouse...is a migratory agricultural worker or a migratory fisher...who has moved within the past thirty–six months from one school district to another to enable the...family to obtain temporary or seasonal employment in an agricultural or fishing activity (New York State Migrant Department of Education, 1998, p.1)

Migrant children's families are employed in farm and farm–related activities that include the harvesting of plants, the production of vegetables, the production of poultry and milk, ranch activities, working in fisheries, and working at activities related to the cultivating of trees. Many adolescent children of migrant families work alongside their parents, where they are exposed to physical risks that the United States legal system protects "majority" adolescents from in the form of child labor law.There is little research that chronicles the lives of migrant workers and their children, although anecdotal reports suggest that "the lifestyles and living conditions of these families place the children at high risk for numerous...problems." Poverty, exposure to pesticides, lack of clean drinking water, and interrupted schooling are among the most damaging factors that work to contribute to these children's social, emotional, and health–related problems, such as a high incidence of tuberculosis, parasitic disease, and iron deficiency (Miller, Gordon, & Kupersmidt, 1995). Of course, any socio–emotional challenges are exacerbated by the changes brought about by adolescence as they intertwine with the larger societal issues of race, gender, and class.

Migrant families view education as "their children's way out of the cycle of migrancy and...have a high respect for the teacher's professional opinion" (Diaz, Trotter, & Rivera, 1989). "Yet, there is a paucity of research describing migrant children in school settings (and in particular, their literacy and language learning), even though, like other children, they are required by law to attend school until they reach 16 years of age. Sadly, what the research does indicate is that even though migrant families care very much about their children's education, "the duration of migration was significantly related to dropping out," and that *close to 80%* of migrant Mexican American adolescents do, indeed, drop out of school (Hinojosa & Miller, 1984).

The duration of these adolescents' migration obviously has devastating effects on their educational progress. Migration itself places enormous roadblocks on their learning in a traditional American school setting. Beginning school more than 30 days late, learning a second language (or in the case of rural migrant Mexican students, a third language), experiencing differing academic expectations, societal and institutional racism, and erratic access to community services places most of these multiply–marginalized students at an impossible juncture: school versus dropping out. Like other adolescents who are multiply–marginalized, these students, too, shut themselves off from the public arena of school and schooled literacy, resisting and refusing altogether.

School was not the only arena where migrant workers and their families experienced the daily challenges of low expectations and exclusion. In the communities in which they lived, worked, and conducted daily chores or errands, racism hung in the air like a dark cloud from which they knew they could never really emerge—threatening always to burst—at school functions, local bars, and even in grocery store lines.

The Local Backdrop: Attitudes and Expectations

The local farmers were well respected in the little towns and villages that dotted the rural landscape of upstate New York. They didn't live in the villages proper, however, preferring to live next to their fields and apple orchards in grand white houses that seemed to be reminiscent of an earlier time in the south. The largest farmer in the area (measured by acreage and sales) displayed his family's wealth and prestige with a showcase compound of living quarters, barns, and stables. Far off into the distance, safely hidden away on a dirt road among the cornstalks that would be "knee high by the 4th of July" were the migrants' homes—here, quite literally, an entire trailer park stretched on along the dirt road by the dozens like one of those endless trailer parks one sees as one drives across the flat plains of the Midwest.

My brothers and I had gone to high school with most of these farmers, and our families were acquainted; both were active in the schools and the community. One farmer appeared larger than life: he was a huge man physically, appearing even taller in boots, blue jeans, and the standard workingman's jacket. At social gatherings, people flocked to him and his two blond–haired daughters to chat or just to be seen. They exuded what we had all been taught to believe about the quintessential American family: beauty, confidence, success, and decency. But there was a dark side to this man, even though his blatant racism—calling fellow high schoolers "niggers" or "nigger lovers"—had been tempered over the years. In front of me, he had become more cautious and more thoughtful of what he said, and I wondered if he weren't simply holding back what he would have really liked to say.

"Lazy" was the first word that came out of his mouth when I asked him about his workers. "Lazy, you can't depend on them for anything. Look, they take their paycheck on Fridays and it's gone on Friday night at the bar." In fact, the ultimate insult, I learned, was to call a white person a migrant: "You're just like them," a friend told me the farmer said to him, "you're just as bad as them, I can't give you your paycheck early 'cause you'll spend the whole thing, too."

Because the migrant workers were portrayed as lazy (despite, of course, toiling in the fields 12–14 hours a day), they were thereby justifiably expendable. This became painfully apparent when the Perez family who had worked in this farmer's fields for over 20 years, was summarily replaced one winter while the Perezes had migrated south to continue working. As the story was told, the Perez family didn't even know until they returned the next season and found their trailers occupied by other families who had been hired to work presumably at a cheaper rate. One of the Perez girls with whom I worked in the migrant summer project wouldn't have been surprised, however; she had told me months before that although the farmer had been good to them, he was racist "just like the rest" and really didn't care much about them. She was right, and I never saw her or the family again.

Regardless of how this farmer and others felt about the migrant workers, however, these workers were becoming a fixture in many places in town. One local bar in particular was becoming notorious for catering to the migrant workers as they, like many men in town, drank beer and played pool on a nightly basis. Curious about whether the migrant workers indeed spent all their money and time drinking and being lazy, I joined in, as an observer, at this Main Street bar.

There were two small bars next to each other on Main Street. Both had been there since I was a little girl and both had always been known as the "old men's" bars. One had remained in the family and had as of late begun to attract the college crowd, while the other had been sold off to a young, white local who, it was rumored widely, looked the other way as drug use went on inside of his bar. And, yet, it was precisely the seediness of this bar that actually seemed to work in favor of the migrant men, because here they were "allowed" in; certainly they wouldn't have mixed well with the college students next door.

Enveloped by thick smoke as I sat drinking a beer and watching and chatting with the patrons one Friday night, I wondered out loud how the migrant men would be treated. Would they be served? Would there be words exchanged? Would there be trouble?

"They don't bother us and we don't bother them," one local told me. "Besides, no one here speaks Mexican."

"Are there ever any fights?" I asked.

"Yea," the local replied, "but usually not between them and us." "They mind their business and we mind ours."

Certain stores, bars, and even corners of the street, I learned, were known as "their" space—spaces where the white townspeople "allowed" the migrant men to congregate, to drink and play pool, or to shop. When a deli opened across the street from the bar, it quickly became a regular hangout for these men and just as quickly became off–limits for most of the rest of the town. But there didn't seem to be much harm done and I was happy to report that it appeared that the migrant workers and the towns-people co–existed, peacefully, at a distance. (In other towns and cities across New York State, an ignorance of what lay beneath such appear-ances has had tragic consequences. For example, on Long Island, two white men were officially charged with attempted murder after they lured two migrant men into an abandoned building, on the pretext of work, and beat them savagely with tire irons and shovels. "Queens Man," 2001. As the story unfolded, many Long Islanders expressed their dismay that what they too, thought, was peaceful co–existence had been, indeed quite the opposite.)

It became clear, however, that the real problem was bubbling just be-neath the surface, a surface where harsh words, fists, and other kinds of violence were usually kept under control. Rather, here, the real (and appar-ent) problem manifested itself in the form of exclusion and silence, of down casting one's eyes, or of segregating. Even though the cloud of ra-cism that hung over the town did not spew physical violence on those be-low, it did burst, often in insidious ways, raining its venom and hatred on all.

A call came to me at my office; the voice on the other end was upset and shaky. "Brett, we need your support. Do you know what they've done at XYZ elemen-tary school? The principal is standing outside and refusing to let the [migrant] kids in the doors. He is telling them that they can't come to school here and other parents from the town are taunting the [migrant] kids and their parents. They don't understand and he [the principal] threatened to call the police." (Fieldnotes, 5/96)

This desperate situation was more typical, I was told, of how migrant workers and their children were treated. When it came to education, in particular, school officials often took matters into their own hands, even when doing so was in flagrant violation of the law. (In New York State, as in many other states around the country, *all* children, regardless of immigration status, i.e., "illegal" or not, are allowed, i.e., required, to attend school. Further, principals have no legal requirement to enforce U.S. immigration laws by keeping children out of school for lack of documentation (School opening alert, 1998.)

As the morning wore on, and members of advocacy groups and the police arrived, the principal finally acquiesced, allowing the children to attend school. The damage, however, had most certainly been done-- disruption, stares from the Anglo kids, name–calling, heads hung in shame. The principal's lack of understanding of the law coupled with his blatant racism had created an environment where the culture of refusal engulfed these children *before* they even entered the building. What was particularly frightening was that this culture was sanctioned by many; the dark cloud of racism hung over the town like a banner of pride. This had been the first day of school for many children, and undoubtedly, the last for far many more.

The Migrant Summer School Program Setting

The Migrant Summer School Education Project is housed in a building that has functioned as the village's Catholic school for as long as anyone can remember. In the summer, the old red brick building takes on a new character as it is transformed into a school for migrant children, worlds apart from the children, who, in uniform and polished shoes, speaking English, sit in the very same seats during the "regular" academic year.

The irony of denying these children an education was particularly salient considering the fact that many of the local rural schools had among the lowest high school graduation rates in the county—often far below the so–called troubled local urban schools (New York State Department of Education, 1995). The Migrant Education Project was originally designed as a "supplement" to the interrupted schooling that migrant children received. The project ended up, however, in many ways to serve as "enrichment" to the local curricula that had simply become non–competitive.

Over the years, many of the same families returned to this rural area to seek farm work, arriving en masse in the spring and remaining well into the fall to harvest apples, squash, and other late–season produce and many of their children, therefore, had attended the local schools over a period of several years. The adolescents, in particular, felt they knew the local school districts well, reporting that it was extremely hard to "catch up" and that it didn't matter because many of the teachers were "racist" anyway. In truth, many of the classroom teachers these students encountered during the school year saw them as "transients" and simply were not able (and in some cases, could not be bothered) to help these students to bridge the gap in their learning. By the time, therefore, that most of the adolescents came to the summer school program they resented school and would have preferred to have been allowed to work along with their parents in the fields despite the long working hours and the socio–physical risks.

During the course of two summer programs, I was a participant observer in the Advanced ESL/English/Reading classroom, the classroom that also served as the eighth and ninth graders' homeroom where many of the work/school students could be found. Ms. Lesa Bo, a certified bilingual (Spanish/English) teacher, was gracious in accepting me as an observer for the summer term.

Program

The Migrant Education Project has been funded by the federal and state government and sponsored by the local university for over 20 years. The program's mission, unwavering throughout the years, is to provide for migrant children "a comprehensive instructional program with [an] emphasis on reading, math, and bilingual education" (State University of New York, 1996, p. 1) while focusing on preserving the linguistic and cultural heritage of the students as well as exploring the "pervasive nature of racism [in society] and its enactment..." (p. 1). Curricular goals were set such that "multicultural and cross–cultural activities [were] designed to deepen appreciation of the children's own culture while developing an understanding of those attributes that are unique to other cultures," while the integration of the reading, writing, speaking, and listening processes was developed in an "intrinsically rewarding" way. Clubs such as the Boy Scouts, Girl Scouts, Chess Club, and Art Club were set up by the program director and run by the teachers each Friday morning. Instructional field trips were planned at least once a week.

The migrant project curriculum is indeed comprehensive, offering courses in math and literature as well as current events and health education to students in grades K–9. In addition, in an effort to bring the adolescent population into school and out of the fields, the project offers a work/school program in which teens earn points and therefore a paycheck by attending school, working in the cafeteria, and/or working with or tutoring the younger children. Small classroom size was the norm at the summer school, with each class of between 10 and 15 students having one teacher and one teacher assistant. Headed by a director who had run the program for well over 20 years and staffed with some extremely dedicated teachers, this migrant summer school program was widely considered (by local universities) to be an innovative, successful model of the ways in which school could truly serve English–language learners' needs.

The adolescent program, housed within the Migrant Education Project, was designed for students in grades seven to nine. Considered a summer program of "work and study," the program included career education, employment skills, and real–world work experience such as tutoring younger students, publishing a newspaper, and assisting in food service. As an incentive to pull adolescents out of the fields and into a school setting, students received nominal pay. Interestingly, despite horrendous working conditions and safety issues in the fields and despite the offer of a clean school, hearty meals, a dedicated faculty, and a forward–looking curriculum, many of the adolescents just bided their time in summer school, waiting for the day when their parents would allow them to work in the fields alongside them and other family members.

And, yet, the migrant summer school program held out the opportunity of success for many of the other adolescents. The program itself was a bold attempt (despite the cloud of racism I described above) to "bridge" the students' education as they moved from place to place and from school to school. Many of the teachers and certainly the director of the program attempted to show these adolescents the true possibilities of school as a place where their lives and experiences, i.e., their local literacies, counted.

And, yet, in many ways the school was little more than a temporary oasis from the realities of being poor, non–English speaking, Mexican, and transient.

Little Change: What Does the Future Hold?

The housing code for migrants in New York State has not changed in close to 30 years (Nieves, 1996, pp. B1, B6). Only recently has a New York law been passed requiring drinking water to be provided in the fields as well as a proposal asking for a phase–out of all outhouses and installation of smoke alarms in all living areas. Hot water still does not have to be provided for dishwashing, and inspections by the State are waived when the workers are in the camps. Indeed, the work that migrant workers do is ranked (along with mining) as the most hazardous. Yet migrant workers are still paid minimum or below minimum wage. Farming remains the number one industry in New York State.

According to Nieves (1996) and stories I have been told firsthand, little has changed for migrant workers over the last several decades, but few of the migrant workers complain for fear of losing their jobs. In the cinder block barracks or trailers where most of the families that I visited lived, conditions were worse than I could ever describe in words here. Why, then, I wondered, would the adolescents, in particular, want to leave school so desperately to live a life like this? What was so horrendous about their schooling experiences that would essentially drive them out of school, into the fields, and into a world of great socio–physical risk? Migrant families remain the hidden, forgotten workers for both New York State's and (one) of the country's most powerful industries. Their children remain hidden, too, silenced students for whom an education is supposed to be guaranteed by law. The battle for the cultural space of the adolescents who live and work under these conditions is all but lost. There is virtually no cultural space left for them anywhere: neither school nor society wants them.

But these adolescents, like all adolescents, find ways to frame their lives and their experiences. They attach meaning to their particular experiences and create literacies around their lives, validating each other and their alternative cultural spaces and places together. The culture of refusal acts as a profound mechanism by which these adolescents can cope with their being shut out of the central public spaces of school and society, as they resist, refuse, and, ultimately, disappear into the fields altogether.

In the next chapter, I will discuss the places and spaces in which incarcerated adolescents lived, worked, and went to school. Different from the migrant kids in many ways (e.g., race, geographic origin, and language heritage), these adolescents share a perception by society that they, too, are expendable. We will see how these incarcerated adolescents, like their migrant counterparts, disappear altogether—instead of behind the tall cornstalks, behind the cold, stark walls of the jails society builds to keep all the rest of us "safe."

Chapter Six

Bed and Breakfast:
The Incarcerated Youth Program

How do you like our place? the prison guard asked me with a smile. It's a brand new facility, he continued, the walls are just painted, and they even added those windows to the top to let in the light, he said, gesturing upward. They get three squares, an exercise room, and TV. Bed and breakfast is what they should call it...damn free bed and breakfast! (Fieldnotes, 1996).

T he prison guards liked me. They couldn't figure out why I was there at first, but I could tell they liked me. "Woman on the floor," they would yell when I walked down the long, acrid–smelling hall-hallway. They yelled, "woman on the floor," I learned, so that none of the guards would walk their male units when I was in the hallway. They didn't want to risk my being jeered, taunted, or worse yet, they said, spit at.

The smell inside the jail is what I remember first about the place, and it is a memory that will never leave me. Acrid–smelling isn't quite right; it was a stale odor: of body odor, of hair gel, sweat, and must. It was a powerful smell that had never seen the outdoors, a smell that no breeze could ever wash away. It wouldn't have mattered anyway, though, because there were no windows in the facility that opened. The air, like the smell, simply circulated round and round, day after day, like the time. It made one dizzy.

No one ever did spit at me, however, and although a few male adolescents made reference to my sexuality (nothing unusual, I thought, men did that), I found the adolescents to be completely respectful of me. They had learned, quickly, that I was there to help the teachers, a role they figured was as good as one could have. They liked me, too.

It was a different story with those in charge, however. Even though I had been officially cleared by both the school district (who administers the incarcerated youth school program) and the administration for the correctional facilities in the county, I knew I was not welcomed. In fact, right up until the day I left the jail, those in charge at the front desk harassed me.

I had been issued a picture ID authorizing me to be in the facility. However, to gain access to the classrooms and the living quarters of the adolescents, one had to be buzzed through two sets of steel doors. As one entered the building, the first thing you could see was what I called "the command post," a glass (bullet–proof) encased center raised above the ground level ground level of the foyer. In the center sat at least two guards, of superior rank, armed, who controlled all the initial movements of anyone who came through the front door. To the right of the post was the "strip and search" room (a place where relatives and friends of the incarcerated youth were frequently searched); to the left, a room where the secretaries sat. If you had an ID you were supposed to be able to move toward the steel doors, wave your ID, and you would be buzzed in. But even after months of being there, those in the command post refused to buzz me in, making me wait in the same line with the visitors who did not carry such ID.

"What do you do again?" the female guard asked. Even when I learned that "I am a professor" was definitely the wrong answer, and said, "I'm here to help the teachers," I was still harassed. "Well, we'll need more ID, like a license, and you'll have to surrender that here with me." It was a scenario that played again and again, and as I waited, I talked and joked with the other visitors: aunts, girlfriends, and mothers of the boys with whom I worked. I was never "allowed" to work with the female inmates. The staff at the jail claimed it was too difficult: many females were pregnant, "on drugs," or simply "strung out." The females in this institution were even more hidden away than their male counterparts, a phenomenon I discuss more fully in the last chapter. They, however, were always treated worse than I was.

Educational Services for Youth: The Incarcerated Youth Program

Incarcerated youth programs throughout the country are relatively new phenomena, if they exist at all. The reason for this was "common wisdom," I was told: The role of incarceration was a punitive rather than a rehabilitative one, so that few states should (and indeed do) set aside any money for educating their young prisoners at all. In fact, according to research done by the Corrections Educational Research Center (Lewin, 1995), only 21 states require at least some inmates, i.e., those with eighth grade or less, to attend classes. The quality of the classes, however, varies widely, as does the purpose of education as rehabilitation. But the underlying reason most states are reluctant to fund education programs for its prisoners is simply that it is expensive and, therefore, unpopular to its voting population. Ironically, though, research has shown that the cost of educating a prisoner is often one–third the cost of incarceration (Boyce, 1994; Lewin, 2001). These same studies also show that inmates who are educated (while in jail) have a far less recidivism rate than those who are not. In fact, 80% of inmates who earn four–year college degrees while in prison never return to jail. And, yet, as incarceration rates rise dramatically around the country, spending on education in the institutions themselves is on the decline.

In New York State, "schooling" for adolescents in jail settings has only been mandated since 1988. Prior to that education was not seen as a necessary component to one's ability to "rehabilitate," and it certainly was not seen as a right of the incarcerated. The notion that "bad" people should get something for "free" (or at taxpayers' expense) was not a popular one. After all, a prison guard told me when we talked about college courses being offered to inmates, "I paid for my [college] education, why should they get theirs for free?"

In states where incarcerated youth must be offered an education, prisons are usually mandated to do so under statutory authority. In New York State, for example, the law falls under both Correction Law, 45(6) and Education Law, 3202 (7) which states:

> Section 7070.1. Policy. In cooperation with the appropriate school district, each local correctional facility shall provide all eligible youth the opportunity to participate in educational services pursuant to section 3202(7) of the Education Law. Eligible youth are entitled to receive such educational services and shall be encouraged to become involved in an educational program provided by the school district so that they may obtain those skills and credentials necessary to function more productively both during incarceration and after release. (Educational Services for Youth, Statutory Authority, 1998)

Eligible youth are defined as "an inmate who is under 21 years of age and has not yet received a high school diploma and...has been incarcerated in a local correctional facility for 10 or more calendar days."

Data show (Lewin, 1995) that New York State spends more than any other state on education and educational resources (around $50 million) for its incarcerated youth. This spending was mainly a result of massive budget increases allocated to help the system deal with the threefold increase in the prison population. However, the spending was seen, in part, as a reaction to recent studies (mentioned above) that cite lower recidivism rates for educated prisoners than for those who are not given the chance to participate in an education program while incarcerated.

The Program

New York State allows for the school district (in the county in which a jail exists) to plan, develop, and provide faculty and staff for its incarcerated youth programs. The jail administration, on the other hand, provides the inmates and the classroom space as well as providing the security, discipline, and restraint deemed necessary to carry out a successful program.

The purposes of the two institutions would seem to be at odds: one provided the tools so that the inmates could "rehabilitate" so that they could express themselves in an educational setting previously out of their reach, to feel a sense of accomplishment amidst the chaos around them; while the other provided the tools so that the inmates could "repent" so that they could pay for their crimes over and over again as they were reminded by the white, middle–class guards that they were black, Latino, poor, uneducated, and expendable.

The purpose of education was perceived differently inside the jail classrooms. Indeed, the youth program itself seemed to embrace many of the goals of the prison an institution, including the "eradication" of certain behavior as a prerequisite to learning. This was clearly reflected in the program's mission statement:

> the behavior of a student and his/her academic performance comprise a well established relationship. While our emphasis…is behavior modification, designed specifically to impact the student in such a way that the motivation for his/her offensive behavior becomes, *extinct*, the ultimate goal is an increase in student performance. In short [we are committed] to eliminating many of the *deficiencies* which impact the lives of the students [emphases mine]. (1998)

In reality, then, a major focus of the program was on making "extinct" the students' behavior—behavior, incongruent with the school expectations that were presumed to have caused the student to "fail" in the first place. Of course inherent in this assumption was that no learning could take place until the student behaved in such a manner as to meet the prison expectations. But there was a catch to the privilege of this so–called rehabilitative education—it was offered at a price that was contingent upon the will and discretion of much more powerful others.

The teachers faced enormous physical, logistical, and psychological obstacles in providing a suitable classroom environment for these students. Not only did they have to come up with creative solutions for not being able to use pencils and pens (potential weapons), for example, or to attempt to have some quiet time during instruction, sandwiched between moveable, cardboard–like walls, they also had to explain and legitimize themselves as professionals, in general, on a daily basis. In fact, one teacher told me in no uncertain terms that they (the teachers) had to "bend" to the jail administration and that the administration itself was very "anti–teacher," "secretive," and "suspicious" of any outsiders, including them. This sense of hostility fueled the already low opinions by others toward these particular teachers. The assumption that only the "worst" teachers in the district would take this job or were assigned this position was one held by the other teachers in the district, by some of the student–inmates themselves, and even by my colleagues at my then–department of education. These opinions were spoken about openly, often contributing to what I saw as a self–fulfilling prophecy. That is, the more powerless these teachers felt, the more ineffective and disinterested they often became in the students' education. "It's a losing battle" and "they can't learn" were typical statements I overheard some of the teachers make, as they quietly became, I thought, resigned to the fact that the challenges were indeed insurmountable. Worse yet was the reality that this resignation had become insidious; an unspoken "rule" that was perpetuated by the arrogant "I told you so" gazes of the prison guards.

And yet, as in classrooms everywhere, here, too, were teachers who believed in the promise of education, whether it be transitional (as in the migrant program) or rehabilitative, as it was regarded here. The teacher of the "Pre–GED" class, in particular, felt that having such a "captive" (her pun, not mine) audience afforded both her and her students opportunities that had never been presented in their public school educations, such as sustained time for art and drawing, poetry writing, and both skills–based and creative practice on the computer. (This teacher had three computers per the 12 to 15 students in her class, and was always quick to remind me that that was a far better ratio of computers per students than these young men had ever had in their public school classrooms!)

The Curriculum and an Innovative Teacher

The behavioral expectations set forth by the jail administration seemed to spill over into the objectives and implementation of the curriculum as well, specifically in the area of literacy. Here, as in "regular" school, expected literacy outcomes were measured by standardized assessments, such as the GED, but unlike "regular" school were also pre–defined and predetermined by other performance measures, such as the "Test of Adult Basic English (TABE). Before even being allowed into the jail classrooms, the students were tested on a range of skills and knowledge, including language (e.g., grammar, spelling, and sentence structure or syntax, reading and writing, which looked at, primarily, low–level skills such as subject–verb agreement). For example, a score of 6 out of 12 (representing grade level) was necessary to enter the GED classroom. Ironically, the expectations for behavior seemed to match the expectations for basic English language skills: students were to follow rules (both social and grammatical) unquestioned, in their quest to attain mastery and, hence, success. In reality, then, while jail education was touted as rehabilitative, it was, in fact, as punitive as many of the other programs that the jail as an institution sanctioned.

There were two official classrooms inside the jail: the GED class and the Pre–GED class. (Other support activities took place in other areas, including tutoring services to those confined to their cells, writing workshops after school hours, and ESL resource.) Yet the GED and Pre–GED classrooms remained the center of the inmates' educational opportunities. And school was required.

The Pre–GED classroom teacher had a very intimidating air about her. She studied people, and she had studied me, both closely and at a distance, until she had decided whether I was who and what I purported to be. As she told me later, "I just wanted to make sure we were on the same page." In truth, she needed to know that I had the same level of commitment toward these adolescents and toward her and the enormity of the tasks that lay ahead of both of them. She cared deeply about what she did, and it showed.

The curriculum of the Pre–GED classroom was much less prescribed than that of the GED classroom even though both teachers in essence taught the same subjects, including math, science, social studies, and language arts (although in the GED class, this component was aptly called "grammar"). Much of the difference in the two classrooms centered on the teachers themselves: their overall demeanor and attitudes, their view of rehabilitative education and the inmates, and even what constituted (or should constitute) schooled literacy. For those reasons (and the fact that the nature of the Pre–GED classroom allowed me to form relationships with the students), I observed far more frequently in the Pre–GED classroom, and over time I became a regular fixture in the Pre–GED classroom.

The Future of Education as Rehabilitation: Bed and Breakfast Part II

There is talk in New York State that the governor is going to ease the "no tolerance" drug laws that have served to incarcerate vast numbers of non–violent, low–level drug users and dealers at unprecedented rates (The details of this proposed bill were released in a *New York Times* article by McKinley 2001, entitled, *Proposals for Overhaul of New York Drug Laws*).) This, then, of course would empty the State's jails of an entire group of minority adolescents: an uneducated, unwanted group of young men, who without the necessary tools to enter mainstream culture, are at an enormous risk of returning to jail, where many of them will, quite literally, spend their entire adult lives.

The "culture of refusal" has taken a strong hold on these adolescents. They have been rejected from school and from schooled literacy and have found ways, in dropping out and in forming alliances both in and out of jail, to survive. Can "rehabilitative education" change this? If we were to begin to implement a curriculum that is not focused on low–level skills (drill and kill), but rather is focused on the local literacies of these young men, would we be more successful in helping them to navigate mainstream society? Should the public schools that serve these children serve them better? Should they serve them equally and with the same respect that they reserves for their more affluent, white population? Should schools of education better prepare teachers for the reality of working with all students, in developing a more "culturally-responsive" teaching approach that includes as a major tenet the importance of including students' local literacies into the discourse of the classroom? We will return to these and other crucial questions in Chapters 8 and 9, but first, in the next chapter, Chapter 7, I will share some of the local literacies of particular migrant students and students in the jail classrooms. It is here that they weave their hopes, dreams, challenges, and resistance and refusal into their stories. And yet, it is also here that we begin to understand the amazing beauty, sadness, and complexity of their lives, their literacies and, hence, our roles as teachers, teacher educators, parents, and members of this society in the 21st century.

Chapter Seven

Local Literacies: Stories from the Fields and the Jails

Can't be a lawyer if you're a nigger...
(Terrell, personal communication, 1998)

Terrell and I were talking about career choices. Terrell was excited about continuing his education at the local community college when he got out of jail, although he feared that there wasn't much available for kids "like him." I met Terrell the first day I came to the jail. He was standing in front of one of the classrooms, talking to the teacher, and when I came in, he moved immediately toward me with his hand out for me to shake. Quite frankly, I was taken aback. I certainly didn't expect "these" kids to have the wherewithal to walk right up to an adult (a white adult), extend his hand, and introduce himself. If I had closed my eyes, Terrell and I could have been playing out this scene in one of the affluent white schools nearby, where this kind of behavior, I thought, probably occurred on a regular basis.

Terrell had learned to play the game—a game he knew was a prerequisite for his attempts at entering "mainstream" society: to have successfully engaged with "schooled literacy" to receive his GED degree; to have learned to speak to adults (teachers, guards) as politely and deferentially as possible; and even to try out the use of what "mainstream" society might describe as "impeccable" manners in welcoming a newcomer like me into the classroom. Terrell, it would seem, had shed the vestiges of the culture of refusal, successfully becoming the kind of adolescent society may someday label "model."

Prison personnel would say that they had "rehabilitated" Terrell; that the "change" that manifested itself both in his behavior and in his schoolwork was reflective of an effective prison program designed to do just that. And there was tangible proof, too: Terrell, they pointed out, began to write about his experience of finding "truth," something he could not have done without having come to jail in the first place. In one of his final essays for his GED teacher, Terrell writes:

I am most proud of getting a chance to learn more and coming to reality and finding out the truth about life. If I wouldn't have never came to jail, I would never found out the quality of life. And about school, one thing I'm proud of is taking my GED test and I feel real good to know that I accomplished one of my goals. Another thing I was proud to find out was knowledge is infinite.

Despite these outward appearances, however, Terrell was still acutely aware of who he was and how he would be received as he left the jail, GED in hand, to attend classes at the local community college. When I pressed him, privately, to tell me more about his career aspirations, he was quick to list off any number of jobs that he, as a Black male, would have difficulty getting. "Can't be a lawyer if you're a nigger," was not only a matter–of–fact statement, to Terrell, it was, simply, a statement of truth.

The Literacies of Rehabilitation

Like Terrell, many of the adolescents with whom I worked had found ways, when necessary, to fulfill the expectations of white, middle–class society, both through their behaviors and in their schooled literacies. For example, Victor Nunez, a 17–year–old English Language Learner (ELL), practicing writing an essay for an upcoming GED test in his jail classroom, wrote:

"Why honesty is the best policy"
I agree with being honest...Out in the world people lie about everything. Man cheating on girls, girls cheating on man. The only thing it leads up to is the girl or boyfriend finding out and that's when the fighting begins. People even lie about being married, having kids in their lives, or the crimes they committed.

Here, Victor makes clear the effects of rehabilitation on his life: honesty—a solid, American mainstream virtue—is indeed the best policy. And yet, Victor's voice and the experiences (i.e., the local literacies) of his life are still very much a part of how he expresses himself; how he relates to the concept of "honesty"; how he, therefore, relates to the world.

The White, male adolescents in the jail classrooms (albeit, making up fewer than 1% of the inmates) were also anxious to express an "expected" new hope for their lives. For example, Ryan, 16 and one of the few Anglo adolescents I ever saw in either one of the jail classrooms at any time, writes clearly about his repentance and newfound understanding of what it takes to be a member of "mainstream" society (Ryan's work is left in its original to highlight his struggle with the conventions of schooled literacy).

I now realize how much my thinking allwys gets me into the werst problums and sichonations [situations]. I wont to go home so bed. Some time when I think about what I have done I get angry, hort, discusted, and disapointed with my self. But I have to exept it eavin [even] if I dident want to I have no uther chose [other choice]. I just have to reamember this when I do get realeast [released]. I have to remember that seling drug is not worth it.

Ryan's inability to use the conventions (i.e., "correct" grammar usage and syntax) of standard English reflects not so much resistance and refusal as it represents a lack of knowledge and/or access to the conventions themselves. Like his story that reveals a regretful young man, both his experiences (although peppered with tales of drugs and violence) and his language use are matched more closely to that of white, middle–class society. There is, therefore, a profound difference in how Ryan describes his hopes for the future. When asked, he is upfront and very poignant about it: "I got a much better chance, you know. I'm White." Indeed, Ryan has a far better chance of entering mainstream society (and thereby becoming "successful") simply because he is White. The simple conventions of schooled literacy can be learned.

Like their lives, these adolescents' literacies were statements of truth that, when necessary, were neatly matched to and beautifully enmeshed in mainstream society's perceptions and expectations. Schooled literacy was a game these kids could play—a script that could be learned and repeated, when necessary. And yet, sadly, it was through their local literacies that we learned the "truth" about them; of the peripheral status of their lives and the diminished expectations they had about becoming "successful" and happy adults, equal partners in a society that continued to see them as different, dangerous, and unreachable.

The Literacies of Resentment

Playing the game was something that the adolescents in the migrant summer school classrooms were skilled at as well, although, it seemed, not to the degree that the students in the jail classrooms were. Many of the jailed adolescents had realized, early on, that their lives would be much easier (both in and out of jail) if they repented their sins, accepted jail and school as the institutions that could help them become more successful, and simply followed along. The migrant adolescents, on the other hand, saw school as unimportant and they resented having to waste valuable time to learn to read and write in a language (i.e., English) that for them was not a central focus of their lives. The institution they relied on most was firmly by their side: family. Many of these students found that toiling with (and thereby, being with) their families in the fields was far more rewarding and satisfying than working within an institution that not only treated them with disdain, but also was ill–equipped to deal with the interrupted nature of their schooling.

For many of the students in the adolescent classes, themes of outward resentment toward school stood out clearly. Laura, a very bright girl from Mexico, noticeable immediately by her long, jet–black hair and beautiful smile, had been coming to this small town with her family most of her life. As a result, she had spent most of her schooling experience splitting time between schools that, in her words, were "not made for me." When asked to put her thoughts down on paper about school in general, Laura had this to say:

> My life suck
> Life such in school because there are many thing I do not want to do but I have to.

Limited by her "formal" knowledge of writing, as well as an acute understanding that her writing did not match schooled literacy, Laura summed up her feelings in one sentence. When asked to elaborate, she simply said, "Why, it doesn't matter anyway!"

And yet, as I got to know Laura and some of her other classmates, I learned that it did matter. For example, in an informal peer conference group, in which the students had been encouraged to talk about some topics for their writing, Laura revisited the story of why she hated school, looking, in effect, for validation (and hence elaboration) on the theme. This is how the conversation unfolded:

Brett: Why do you want to go back to the fields?
Mary: Men, well one is cute, but he has long hair, it's like up to here.
Laura: You don't like that or you do like that?
Angie: He's cute, but his hair's gotta go. I don't like a man having longer hair than I do [lots of laughter].
Laura: And the other one is all lazy, you know when we're planting the things, the [stalks] have to go in this thing, you know and the machine is moving and, they fall and he has to run and get 'em and put 'em back on there, and he is so lazy.
Mary: I ran out of plants, right Saturday, I ran out of plants, and he was talking with the other one 'cause and they are always getting in to arguments, and I'm there and taking my…they are talking…mom's plants 'cause I ran out of them and so he seen it, he's like, "Oh, I gotta go, and so he ran over there and got me some plants.
Brett: Whose farm is it?
Mary: It's this lady's farm, I don't know her name.

Brett: So, will they pay you cash? Like sixty dollars.
Angie: No, check—on Friday.
   Laura: Every Friday.
   Mary: My mom checks them...I went on Monday through Thursday, I got a forty-eight dollar check and on Saturday I got a fifty-two dollar check!
   Brett: Wow, that's a big difference!
   Angie: So for one day how much did you get?
   Mary: Fifty–two dollars but we worked 'till four!
   Brett: So how long will it last, though, I mean the planting, and...
   Mary: Three weeks, then we gotta get the wheat out of the cabbage.
   Laura: And that's not hard either...
   Brett: So your moms are gonna let you do this? Quit summer school and go to...
   Mary: She doesn't want me to come here.
   Brett: (To Angie) And your grandma?
   Angie: (Shakes her head "yes.")
   Mary: And I think it's better going to work anyway 'cause you get to buy yourself more clothes...

The conversation in this peer group really served as a forum in which these migrant adolescents could not only explain to me the centrality of the particular experiences in their lives, but could also seek validation among themselves (and me) that what they had to say was indeed interesting, exciting, and even valuable. Offered as a window to their worlds, this conversation highlighted the detailed workings of their lives—from running out of plants to putting the stalks of the plants into a machine, to not liking men with long hair—these girls' local literacies became framed in *their* everyday lives.

Many more of the migrant adolescents' local literacies, however, could only be told directly out of the fields: from the homes where they lived and cared for younger siblings while their parents worked in the orchards or in the fields.

Javier, a wisp of a boy, had not been to summer school in a number of days. He had to repeat third grade last year, and Colleen, his ESL teacher, was worried that he would at this young age drop out of school altogether. Worse yet was the fact that his older sister (a "vulnerable" seventh grader named Maria), too, had not been seen. My fieldnotes of a visit to their home follow:

Once again, Colleen takes me for a ride, this time to the trailer where Javier and Maria live with their family. As we pull up to the trailer door (again far out in the country), we see Javier and Maria's father sitting on the lawn tieing his shoe—hat on—empty beer cans and rum bottles all around him. He is embarrassed. As Colleen asks why the kids have not been in school, Maria opens the door, holding it with her hip, as she greets us with a bushel of freshly–picked tomatoes cradled in her hands.(There is something about the smell of freshly picked tomatoes. It is earthy and spicy all at once. That is the problem with store–bought tomatoes or frozen tomatoes—they lose most of their smell and therefore, I think, most of the original flavor.) We each take a tomato, and in proper form when someone on a farm offers you a freshly picked apple, or string beans, or in this case, tomatoes, we begin to eat them right there—raw, with the red juice happily running down our chins. It is only now that Maria is ready to talk to us. (An approximate translation of a fast-moving dialogue in Spanish follows)

Javier can't come back to school. We had to switch trailers 'cause the other guy worked here longer and so he gets the good trailer. So, he'll switch schools again. And besides, Javier has asthma, so I must stay home to help. And [our] father can't take Javier to school. He loses an hour of work [a day] leaving and coming back from the fields to drive us to the bus. And we only have five weeks left and then we go back to Texas. I'm sorry.

But Maria did come back to school (at least one more time) and when I pressed her to tell me more about her life and her experiences with schooling and with the literacies expected of her in school, she replied unequivocally:

I really hate it. And I really hate writing about it. Sometimes I get really sad and depressed. It's torture time [school]. Our mother wants us to keep on with Spanish. I started in fourth grade here—before we was in Mexico—then Texas—now back to New York. We speak Spanish at home and my mother gets mad if they [brothers and sisters] speak English at home. I've been to four or five different schools. I'd like to take art. But it's torture.

The literacies of the adolescents in the jail classrooms also revealed their resentment toward school; however, the resentment seemed to be couched differently. For example, many of the jailed adolescents admitted that they had actually liked school (i.e., during their public school experience prior to coming to jail) and that it had been a combination of outside factors (mostly gang and drug–related) that contributed to their "failure" in school. In other words, the jail kids, for the most part, saw *themselves* as the failures, while the migrant kids saw the *school* as the ultimate failure.

I met Robert as he came straggling into the pre–GED classroom late one morning. The teacher later told me that he had originally refused to come (but was eventually "forced" to—remember school is required for jailed adolescents in New York State). This had really surprised the teacher because he always came to class "early and very enthusiastic." Robert, a 17–year–old African American, was "slow," she told me (his mother had been a crack addict and he had suffered the consequences) and probably had become discouraged about their talk a few days before about how difficult college might be for him. Robert often got discouraged, the teacher told me. And he rarely got the extra help or attention he needed during his public school education. "He was just one of those Black, special needs kids who slipped through the cracks," she explained. And he knew it.

When I asked him about school, Robert told me that he had "done really well" and had "really liked school," and blamed himself for falling prey to the violent atmosphere of a tough, urban school:

> I didn't get in trouble till I went to the city, then I started fighting to protect myself. Then I just brought a gun every day, but I got caught doing that. I liked my teachers there [names three of them] it wasn't their fault. Then I had to go to the other school [the alternate school for kids kicked out of the public system] and I still carried my gun and never got caught. There was this one teacher there who was always in my face, making fun of me. So, I called him "Gaymeister" and I took him to the supply room and threatened to kill him and I pushed him. I paid my girlfriend to smash his hood and then I ended up here on a drug trafficking and gun charge.

Other of the young men, too, talked and wrote about school:

> Marlin: School's great, don't let anyone tell you it's school and all that. They try to pretend it's the school's fault. It's not.

> Marcos: Just like he said, I liked school. I took ESL and the white teacher was good. School's fine, it's fun, but you gotta go through the streets to get to school.

> Sal: It's a tough life. To fit in you have to be bad, to belong, to be like somebody. I really liked school. Every little thing they said. Here, you gotta be real forgiving.

Yet, even as these adolescent males wrote about their failures rather than the school's, they still resented what school represented: an institution to which, for the most part, they had been denied access; an institution that did not reflect their realties nor their lives; an institution, therefore, that they could easily resist and refuse altogether.

The Literacies of Refusal

"I only got three more chickens left before I don't have to listen to this shit anymore," Ben said. The young men in the jail marked the time until their "outdates" (the day they would actually leave jail) by the number of Sunday chicken dinners they had left. "Three more chickens" was a cause for celebration; with good behavior Ben might actually avoid the red tape confusions and delays for which institutions like jails are notorious, and be released before having to eat a fourth chicken.

Ben was visibly unhappy as the GED teacher began class by having all the students take out a pencil to prepare to write. There were loud groans and a lot of cursing heard: "Fuck this class. We go on the streets and take this!" Ben, like the rest of the students, who had begun a collective whine, must know something I didn't.

And they did. The GED teacher continued her monologue at the front of the room. Like dutiful inmates, however, most of the students settled down, having had sufficient time to vent—pencils poised to blank sheets of prison–issue lined paper. The teacher continued:

> We're going to do a literature lesson today on style and structure, formal and in-
> formal. Now, pay attention because this is something you need to get on with your
> life—formal style and diction. So, on your paper, tell me what these mean: 1.
> style, 2. diction, 3. figurative language, and 4. tone.

"Fuck this," I hear coming from the young man who had said "fuck this class" just moments before, as he turns to me and asks, "Are *you* going to teach us anything?" "No, not today," I reply, I'm just gonna hang out." "Cool," he says," 'cause this is another dumb–ass question—fuck this school."

As much as these adolescents were astute at playing the game, matching the stories of their lives to the expectations of school and society, they were also very astute at rejecting the game entirely. After all, they knew that, in reality, the game was one in which they were not players; they stood alone, yet together, rejected as the "leftovers" that the captain of the team never picks as he chooses up sides.

Not all of the adolescents were as forthcoming as the young man who understood that "style" and "diction" really had no bearing on his life, and yet, they were still quite expressive. In fact, many of the students were very vocal about the mismatch between what they were expected to learn in school and their lives, both past and future, and their complaints indeed seemed to carry merit.

For example, when the GED teacher decided to incorporate the theme of "resume and essay writing" into her daily writing lessons, the young men questioned, once again, her insistence that these were skills that they needed in order to become successful in the world. In some very creative moments, in fact, rather than writing about the topic "Do you feel educa-

tion is the passport to the future?" the boys debated not only the actual usefulness of the skill itself (i.e., essay writing), but also the relevance of the
specific question she expected them to write about. Following are some of
their reactions:

In response to the usefulness of resume and essay writing, Roger wrote:

> What good is writing an essay do for me out in the world? What would it accom-
> plish for me? I'll buy me a resume...makes no difference.

And Jorge added,

> Don't need to write. I'll hire a secretary. She'll write that I say.

Interestingly, when asked, both Jorge and Roger told me that, in reality,
having a well–written resume would make no difference anyway (in their
prospects of getting "good" jobs), so that learning the skill was "twice as
useless."

The specific question that the GED teacher assigned, "Do you feel education is the passport to the future?" was also met with resistance. In fact,
an extensive conversation ensued among some of the adolescents, first
about their reasons for not wanting to rewrite what they had written (especially that they should find something nice to say about education and its
positive impact on their futures), and then that a different question altogether might be more appropriate:

> Why write it over? What's wrong with it? I'd rather change the question—like
> Malcolm X said, if you get an education, it's a *tool* for the future. If I had the
> education they had (e.g., Malcolm X and his followers), I sure wouldn't be sitting
> here writing this essay.

As revealing as these adolescents' literacies of resentment and refusal
were, especially to us as educators and to our developing appropriate and
relevant curricula (see Chapter 10 for a fuller discussion on implications
for teachers), other students' stories that made up their culture of refusal
revealed a more troublesome twist: despair. Many of these adolescents'
lives had simply been engulfed by this despair and, when unearthed, could
alternately be seen as hopelessness, depression, withdrawal, and/or anger
and violence. The despair of their lives, revealed in their literacies, was
simply pervasive.

The Literacies of Despair

One young man, Ramon, 17, who, like most of his jailed peers, was doing time for drug possession, when asked to participate in one of the lessons on essay writing, quietly, with his head down, wrote:

> My mother jumped out the window when she was pregnant with me...don't want much to do with this...[writing].

Ramon, I learned, was a deeply sensitive, thoughtful, yet frightened young man. More often than not, however, when I was at the jail to work and visit with the kids, Ramon was in "the box." "Ramon's in the box again, he had three fights over the weekend!" was frequently the explanation I was given by his peers when I asked where he was for class. (Being in the box or being sick were the only valid excuses for missing school—remember that school as rehabilitation was required).)

I was never allowed near "the box" and despite descriptions from the other inmates about what the box was really like (solitary confinement to a cell that was separated from the pods or living areas of the other inmates), the only image I could conjure up was one similar to the "box" that the prisoners of war were kept in the movie *The Bridge over the River Kwai*. And in fact, after talking to both a prison guard and Ramon, I'm not sure the differences were so stark.

Ramon was routinely put in the box and left there for entire weekends and even though the fights weren't always Ramon's fault, a guard confided in me that it was just easier to lock him up for the weekend. The guard explained: Getting "rid" of Ramon would entail fewer explanations, fewer reports to write up, and, therefore less work and fewer problems. Ramon was simply a liability to an "easy" shift, and so, Ramon was often "punished" simply for the sake of it.

Ramon, showing little emotion, explained to me matter–of–factly his interpretation of one of the weekend incidents: "Yea, if I had been out in the street, I would of shot 'em. Not killed them, but shot `em, you know in self–defense. But they [the guards] won't report me and take time away [from his outdate—the day he is to get released]. They [guards] know it was their [other inmates'] fault. But, yea, so anyway, the sarge brought me out and banged my head against the wall, then he used the handcuffs and all just to take me to the box."

Ramon had grown up being punished just for the sake of it. Living in a home with a father who was, according to Ramon, both a "woman beater and a kid beater," Ramon lived in constant fear that his father would, on occasion, actually come home from work on Friday nights only to beat him, his mother, and his siblings and to cause his mother, in a desperate attempt to get away from the abuse, to jump out of a two–story window, pregnant and hysterical. Indeed, life had been very difficult for Ramon, his social worker and tutor explained (Ramon, like all other adolescent inmates, is provided with a tutor during the time he is in the box), and as a consequence, they believed he had become clinically depressed, angry and on occasion, extremely violent. Ramon had become so attuned to his own needs and capabilities, however, his social worker claimed, that he would actually volunteer to go into the box (for a weekend, for example) because he knew that, without his medication and proper treatment, he would be unable to control his temper. She continued:

> This is definitely not the place for him...because he just can't get what he needs here. He can't even get his meds, and the counseling available is, well, unavailable. He'll just get worse here.

Ramon's understanding of himself and of the family and world in which he had grown in was, indeed, remarkable. As I got to know him better (he wouldn't talk to me at first because he said I looked like a "narc"), his life unfolded through both his oral and written literacies in unbelievably sad and disturbing ways.

Ramon talked a lot about his upbringing in disjointed, almost surreal, ways. It was as if he wasn't even sure he had really been there and he jumped around from incident to incident when he tried to describe just what had actually transpired. A sample follows:

> There were tons of us at home, I had six brothers and five sisters. My father got paid on Fridays and never came home from work. When he did, he talked shit all the time, what a punk. I needed my father as a role model, if a father says not to fight...that's why I got into all fights, 'cause my father wasn't there for me. I would just look at my mother like...I wouldn't listen...with a father, he'd kick your ass...hard for kids to say "you not with that."

Ramon related his upbringing to his own slow start in taking responsibility for his family.

> When I had my son, it changed my way of thinking—didn't want him, I was still in school, no job. My cousin, he helped me out, I was working at the car wash, and the mom was taking care of the clothes and school. But, yea, my cousin went upstate [to a maximum security prison] and he just had a baby and didn't even get to see him. He had got a paid lawyer, so he would have gotten worse. After two

kids, I just started smoking cocaine. It had really hurted me when I had found out
my mother smoked the pipe...

And, yet, even in Ramon there was a glimmer of hope. Just before his release date, he talked to me about "learning to take care of his children" and
of wanting to attend the School of the Arts, where a female cousin of his
went and was very happy and successful. In fact, the last time we talked,
Ramon presented me with his first written piece, entitled, "My Life," adding verbally that going to the School of the Arts might be the best thing for
him:

Maybe I could stay out of trouble there—you know it's a school for art, cooking
classes, and theater.

Little did he know, however, that he was not allowed in any public school
in the city; the district had "banned" him—in essence reinforcing a culture
of refusal that they, as an institution, created for him—a culture from
which, effectively now, Ramon had no escape.

Unfortunately these literacies of despair were not limited to Ramon,
and I suspected that many, many more adolescents both in the migrant
summer school program and in the jail would have shared their stories had
they truly believed that any one of us (i.e., teachers, social workers, tutors,
administrators) had created a safe space for them to do so.

M. J., a 20–year–old young man, labeled "borderline mentally re-
tarded" and often called "a big kid in a man's body," was one such student.
But, for him jail it seemed that had become a safe place; a place where he
could talk about himself and his life, a place where he could be the "older
brother," a place where he could reflect and even cry.

M. J.'s life story unfolded to me much like Ramon's did: in bits and
pieces, with powerful images and reflections; sometimes intertwining,
other times bumping up against one another, contradicting themselves in
vivid ways. It was as if both adolescents had never spoken (nor written)
about their lives and themselves before, and as they did they found out
things about themselves that I'm not sure they ever knew.

Like Ramon, M. J. talked a lot about family, who he was now, and who
he envisioned himself to be one day. And also like Ramon, he spoke and
wrote about the deep sadness in his life:

Everyone always told me how dumb I am. I was born in Ohio, we left there when
I was one. Left my father behind. My mother always said I'd be just like him—he
was a bad man—and I never see him—and so when she moved away [his mother

moved south and left M. J. when he was still in junior high school.]. I just got in lots of trouble. I'm not very smart.

M. J. was very much a loner at the jail. He always sat by himself, tucked away at the farthest table in the back of the classroom. None of the other inmates ever sat with him and I had figured that it was because he was so big and powerful–looking that the others were afraid of him. One day, however, as I walked into the classroom, M. J. smiled at me and I decided, nervously, to ask him if I could join him at his table. After that day, I always sat in the back with M. J., where with my most trusted "observer," we both watched the processes of teaching, learning, and life unfold around us.

M. J. kept to himself because he claimed he preferred it that way, and none of the other inmates questioned that. Indeed, he was older and more powerful–looking than most of the other young men in the adolescent program, and he seemed, too, to be at a different place in his life. He was a "thinker," I learned, and he struggled on a daily basis with understanding the notion of "manhood" and "maturity," especially in a world where he had been constantly reminded of how "dumb" he was:

> Yea, I'm in for six months this time, `cause I'm a follower not a leader and being with the wrong crowd. But this time in here has really changed my life, but I feel like I'm dumb, I'm going to be 21...don't have the brains...I'd like to pick up my life, I have so much time...I feel like I'm mature, you know I'm going to be 21...I'm not like some of these kids...

But for M. J., like Ramon, the despair came in overwhelming waves. Even when he had moments, or days of feeling "smart" and sure of himself, the effects of the abuse, the abandonment, and the victimization kept coming back, in real and terrifying ways. When I asked him what he would do and where he would go when he reached his outdate (which occurred when I was there), he told me, with a smile so genuine and a laugh so endearing that he almost fooled me, "Not to worry." He continued, as tears welled up in his eyes:

> Don't worry about me. I'm alone. I don't get visitors, and I don't worry about it...you're the first person who ever "visited" me...I'm alone and that's the way I want it to be...give me time to think.

The deeply disturbing part, once again, was that M. J. was a smart, sensitive, and caring young man, who like countless others in the migrant camps and in the jails, had been labeled and thrown away: by family, school, and a society that perpetuated the horrendous abuse against him, once again aiding in engulfing him in a culture of refusal, while sentencing both his body and his soul to a place from which he could never, and hence would never, escape.

Contrasting Literacies

At first glance, similar literacies of despair seemed to be non–existent among the adolescents in the migrant summer school program. On closer examination, however, it became clear to me that these literacies indeed did exist, but were expressed much differently, seemingly devoid of the deep and pervasive sadness that the jail kids wrote and talked about. The crucial mediating factors that contributed to the migrant kids' stories being more hopeful seemed to be the family, the very subject of their literacies that also caused them so much despair.

Indeed, however striking the contrast between the migrant kids' literacies of despair seemed, they, too, centered around issues of family and loss. For example, during a weeklong exchange in which a number of students and I were working in a writer's circle trying to come up with ideas that were both interesting to them and acceptable to the teacher, some of us engaged in an extended conversation (and subsequent writing activity) around the kinds of things that "hurt" them most in life. (This topic coincided with a theme the students had been working on in health and careers around emotional, physical, and substance abuse, including violence, date rape, and using drugs.) Selena, a seventh grader, who lives with her family in central Florida in the winter and in this small, rural community in the summer, tells me that her family has been hurt by the migratory life they all have had to live, and that seeing any member of her family hurt was the worse thing that could happen. She writes:

> I hate to keep traveling all around `cause it's hard to make friends, and you know my Dad's brother died `cause of it. See, he had cancer and paid lots of money, and the doctors kept taking money and they even checked for AIDS. So my Dad had to sell the car to send money to his mother [in Mexico, where the brother went to recuperate], so he couldn't get here [this season] for work—he went to Mexico and prayed for him [his brother] and then when his brother got better he got back to the States, and he started alcohol and then something burst and he died. It's so sad.

Selena was quick to remind us that it was precisely the strength and closeness of her family that allowed them to get through the crisis. These women, without a doubt, remained the central focal points in Selena's life as they gave her incredible strength and support. Despite incredible obstacles, both obvious (the health of the uncle) and the not–so–obvious (women traveling alone in a country where they have no "legal status" and struggle with the language), these women kept the family together, working and living for survival.

Other migrant kids, though, were not as lucky as Selena. Alfredo, a small kid who looked much younger than the 13 years his records indicated he was, came to summer school, a newcomer this year, from a remote, rural village in what was described to me as the "backwoods" of Mexico. The first thing Alfredo asked for when a bilingual counselor was made available for him was, "Please find my mother."

Alfredo had been separated from his mother a few years back when his father had remarried. Out of school for the same amount of time, Alfredo was moved around these "backwoods" with his siblings, father, and stepmother before coming here for seasonal farm work. Alfredo was having a hard time adjusting, the counselor said, because he came from such a poor area—no running water, few schools, little socialization with others—and he spoke a very pronounced regional dialect that was often unintelligible even to native Mexicans. In fact, it seemed that Alfredo had even developed his own private dialect—an idiolect of sorts—in an attempt either to get the attention he needed, or to separate himself even further from those around him.

Alfredo did not talk or socialize with the other kids in the classroom. It was as if they weren't there. Alfredo drew. He was a prolific illustrator and he drew many pictures of himself surrounded by lots of other people (the counselor reported that these were his older siblings, often the only supervision and the only other "friends" he had). Alfredo, it seemed, had many, many stories to tell, but constrained by his formal ability to write and his reluctance to communicate with anyone else, instead hung his head and drew his life and his literacies, revealing a lonely, sad, child, who I believed desperately missed socialization with others, despite reports to the contrary. To make matters even worse, I thought, was the fact that Alfredo would not return to school in the fall (ending his formal schooling) because he was needed in the fields to work alongside his father and siblings. And so, another voice would be silenced.

And, yet, during the summer that Alfredo was in the migrant summer classroom, the other adolescents became empathetic to his situation, and seemed to give Alfredo voice. The profound sense of loss Alfredo felt and could only express through drawing was an emotion that many of the other kids were sympathetic to, even frightful of; and as the summer wore on, other students became more willing to share these feelings of fear and despair. Laura explained:

I think that it is bad that some kids mothers just live [leave] them when they are young and they don't have any one two turnen [to turn] to. I'll bet that if my mother ever left me I would reather be dead because my family is very important to me.

And Lucy, normally a very quiet young woman, also expressed a sadness in her writing that added to the growing literature in this classroom: the literature and the literacies of despair; literacies that at first glance did not seem to be present at all. Here, as Lucy addresses the topic "Things that hurt me," she writes unabashedly about poverty, drug use, the influence of a grandmother, and her unwavering love for the mother who had abandoned her: (Lucy's writing is left in the original except where meaning may be lost.)

This is Life

When I was first born my grandma took me from my mom because my mom was on Drugs real bad. When I was living with my grandma she did alot for me. when I turned about 6 years old my mom wanted me back so I went to live with my mom for about 1 year but at this time my mom was still on drugs but not as bad. So when I tok my grandma [talk to my grandma] she was still doing drugs. my grandma went to chout [court] to try to take me back.

When I was living in [name of town] and my mom was doing [drugs] she let me do drugs if I wanted too.

So when we went to chourt they just took me they didn't take my little brother. So now I live with my grandma! when my mom moved from...she moved next to me and my grandma. I really love my mom so when she moved next to me I moved back in with her for about 1/2 of a year. Soon as I moved in her new boyfriend moved in. He was nice at frist [first] but when he was living there for a wild [while] he thought he ruled everyone. I didn't like [it] so one day we all got in a Big fight and he told my mom that it was me or him so she picxed him and had a baby by him and than [then] she had the baby he beat her so only my brother and my little sister live with my mom and she gets them eveything and never buys me nothing for Right now. I can't never forgive my mom for puting me out for a Man. I love my mom but I can't forgive Her.

Lucy and the others indeed had made it clear that these literacies did, having been there all the time waiting to be expressed and validated in ways in which the adolescents could feel safe.

Local Literacies and a Culture of Refusal

The local literacies of both groups of adolescents centered around the themes I have highlighted above: rehabilitation, resentment, refusal, and finally, despair. And, yet, even as the many adolescents wrote and talked about their lives within these themes, their literacies were quite different, and the reasons for the crucial distinctions were as varied as the adolescents themselves.

For example, the migrant adolescents wrote and talked about how they resented school, but their resentment seemed to represent a different reality than their incarcerated counterparts. It was as if these adolescents knew and understood that they lived physically, socially, culturally, and linguistically apart from mainstream society and, in most cases, were perfectly content to be in that space. Crucially, even as they refused school and often American "mainstream" society altogether, the importance of family was central and seemed to frame and even perhaps to mediate their resentment.   That is, even though family was important for both groups of adolescents, because the migrant kids traveled with their families (simply by virtue of the nature of their work), their families (even if a mother or a father were missing) were literally living and working together on a daily basis, unfettered, for the most part, from the various curses of American acculturation. The scourge of divorce, violence, and drug and alcohol abuse that often plagues today's American families (from all walks of life) has simply not yet affected these migrant families in the same frightening proportions.

In addition, the migrant kids did not look to formal schooling to define them or lead them down a path to success. The adolescents in the jail classrooms, however, had been well socialized into American culture, believing that they had failed at school, and that, therefore, they would not and could not become successful. The migrant kids, for the most part, saw school as something that had failed them, and they were not as readily willing to blame themselves for the failure of the institution to include them. For the migrant kids, then, family often defined happiness and school was peripheral, while among the jail kids, both the effects of school and family seemed to frame and define their despair.

Of course, there were other mediating factors. First, the challenges of learning a second language and culture (in general much more prominent among the migrant kids) impacted how the migrant adolescents, in general, were able (and willing) to express themselves. In other words, they may have been able to describe their lives in much more detail, had they had the words, quite literally, to do so. And furthermore, the migrant summer school classroom itself was more conducive to kids' needs and to kids' egos, so that, perhaps, while there they simply did not feel the resentment or the despair that the jail kids felt and wrote about on a daily basis. The jail classrooms, for the most part, perpetuated the worst of urban classrooms today—skill and drill exercises, irrelevant curricula, and resentful, even hateful, teachers.

And yet, even in the pre–GED and GED classrooms, there were perceived and real successes of sorts. Students reported that they had "found God," had been given time to think and to reflect, to do art, even to concentrate for the first time in their lives, in a relatively safe environment. Both classrooms, too, gave the students options: at the summer school they could work and/or tutor younger kids; at the jail they could study for their GED and/or prepare for the local community college. Adolescents in both places reported to me that these classrooms were the first places that they had found people who cared (i.e., teachers), and with the relatively small class sizes they now enjoyed and the one–on–one attention they often received, they could, and did, learn.

And, yet, why, then, did such disturbing stories make up so much of the adolescents' local literacies—the stuff of their daily lives and experiences? What kind of society did we live in that young men and women talked and wrote about such fear, sadness, abandonment, and hopelessness?

Indeed, the literacies of despair, like the other literacies that both groups of adolescents shared, are an integral part of a culture of refusal. These multiply–marginalized adolescents are often engulfed by the despair of their lives—a despair we help to perpetuate in both small and large ways, in our families by abandoning them, in our schools by not including them in the curriculum, in our society by our racism, and in our communities by our neglect. As a society, we have disdained and dismissed these kids because they are poor and Black or Latino; we have ignored and punished these adolescents simply for being "multiply–marginalized," hiding them and locking them away. We have, in effect, scripted their local literacies in ways that have led to the culture of refusal to which both groups of adolescents in differing, yet equally poignant and frightening ways, have clearly shown us.

In Chapter 10, I address the very real effect of perpetuating this culture of refusal among all adolescents with whom we work, but particularly among multiply–marginalized adolescents. These adolescents desperately need us, as educators, as parents, and as community members, to put a stop to the institutionalized racism that continues to exclude their literacies (and therefore, them) from mainstream society itself. And finally, in Chapter 10 I talk about the critical implications that such a perpetuation of a culture of refusal will have on us as a society, as teachers, as parents, and as members of a wider "global" community. But first, in the next two chapters, I present "Teacher Literacies." Through the stories of two experienced teachers, I highlight the crucial role the teacher plays in working with stu dents similar to the ones I have described throughout this book. In doing so, I return once again to Ayers' (1997) words that remind us that teaching is, after all, a "matter of love."

Chapter Eight

Teacher Literacies: Stephanie's Option III Classroom

*The dominant school culture functions
not only to support the interests and values
of the dominant society, but also to marginalize
and invalidate knowledge forms and experiences
that are significant to subordinate and
oppressed groups.
This function is best illustrated in the ways
that curriculum often blatantly ignores the
histories of women, people of color, and
the working class.*

(Darder, 1991, p. 79)

Curricular choices are absolutely crucial if we are to teach and learn among the students I have just described (and among all students). In fact, choosing what goes into one's curriculum, even among increased standardardization and accountability, may be the most important decision we make as teachers. Even in places like New York State which have strictly defined aims and objectives derived from content–area standards for the classroom, how we as teachers carry out those mandates through our curricular choices, implementation, and classroom assessment will make the difference as to whether our students (as Stephanie tells us in the following piece) "gather to drink at the fountain."

Throughout this book, I have attempted to represent the adolescents in "their own terms" (refer to Chapter 2 for a fuller discussion) through their own words. Indeed, in many instances the adolescents told me that they wished the whole world could hear and/or read what they had to say. They also wished that the whole world would listen.

And, yet, my representation of their voices has been simply that: one representation. In this chapter and the next, I present the stories of two teachers, Stephanie and Colleen, who, like me, worked and taught with marginalized adolescents—finding, too, entire groups of students who had been rejected from the mainstream culture, retreating into spaces where their voices were never heard or listened to. As I got to know these two teachers better, I realized that they had made those crucial choices about the curriculum: what counted and what did not—choices made for the benefit of their students, not for a district, nor a State mandate. And Stephanie and Colleen, too, wanted to talk and write about these students in ways that presented them positively: in ways that represented hope and success.

In each chapter, I first describe these teachers—who they are, what they teach, and why they continue to teach in challenging circumstances— why they continue to care about students whom many teachers could not care less about. I then present Stephanie and Colleen's stories, leaving their voices intact throughout. Finally, I frame each teacher's literacy within the theme of a "culture of refusal," offering my impressions, perceptions, understandings, and implications of what they have shared with us about their students and the potential impact on all students their curricular choices may indeed have.

About Stephanie

Stephanie was in her mid–20s when I first met her. I remember her vividly because she sat in the front of my first "official" class that I taught as a new Ph.D.; both of us eager and bright–eyed. The class was huge, 35 students, I thought for such an important subject as linguistics, especially at the graduate level, but apparently the college had had no one available to teach the subject in quite a while. I looked around the room and remember thinking, "My goodness, there are a lot of eyes on me. I hope I really do know enough about language to help them in their classrooms."

I figured that Stephanie sat in front of the class to "test" the new professor with her questions. (She later reports that she was "just a first–year teacher trying to make sense of her kids' needs in the classroom.") In fact, she questioned me all the time, reminding me that ESL was not her field (special education was), so that she didn't "get" many of the linguistic concepts I was presenting. But, to Stephanie not "getting" something meant not "getting" something perfect the first time. In fact, Stephanie did understand all of the often tough concepts around language acquisition and language and literacy learning, and brought her perspective of a teacher of children with special needs to the center of our discussions. "Do my kids have the same abilities to learn language?" she would ask. Or, "Why do my kids speak an urban dialect—is there something wrong with that?" Or, "Why is it that my kids can't read or write, if as you say, Brett, most kids can be taught?"

Stephanie tested my knowledge and my experience to their limits. I had had no formal training in special education, and often could not understand why her students were not either developing, or were not appearing to develop either their oral and written literacy skills. And why were the English language learners experiencing the same challenges in both languages? (I learned much later from a bilingual speech pathologist friend of mine that if there is a language "disability" in the second language there must be one in the first—in other words, kids, in reality, don't just struggle in only one language; the brain is equitable in that regard.)

So, we decided to work together. I hired her as our program's graduate assistant and we began to plan our research, writing small grants to get money from the college—yearning to learn the answers to some of our collective questions, and hoping to then be able to share our "findings" with a larger audience.

Stephanie's story opened up my eyes to another new world of students, as I'm sure it will yours. Here, we take a glimpse at another place where kids have been marginalized by their perceived "disabilities" and therefore have resisted and refused to belong to the "space" we call a classroom. The students' disabilities seemed to include not only the "traditional" ones—behavioral, learning, for example, but also ones about which no one would dare publicly speak: color of skin, language, and income level. These were the students' real challenges—challenges that could be overcome, if only momentarily, through the words of poetry and by the encouragement and commitment of a teacher like Stephanie.

Stephanie's Story

To be shut out of the central public space is to be told that one cannot drink the glass of water that lay before her. It is like telling our thirsty selves that there is no water at the fountain. It leaves few alternatives for young people. For, to drink is essential to our survival. Survival is essential to our nature. Therefore, a place to drink will be sought out by those who are denied public access...albeit, an alternative place.

Learning and literacy are mainstream events. They reflect a past history of conformity and expectations for the common good of society. There is almost a communal element to public education. True communication and understanding between the reader, the text, and his or her own voice are extremely difficult to achieve as the goal in education is often to provide a "product" produced simply to contribute to society. This is especially true if the learner is out of the "mainstream," if he or she is of color, or comes from poverty, or exhibits special needs related to behavior and instruction, or in some way is "marginalized" because of his or her difference.

History has always had a tendency to repeat itself and change is slow. These are two "societal" laws with which we, as a nation, must contend.

It is the aim of this chapter to make clear that, while education seems to have evolved over the past centuries, one fundamental issue remains the same and continues to interfere with the success of "marginalized" youth and the schools that allegedly support them. Education as a means to social conformity is the issue that consistently undermines the strength and value of the learner. This chapter highlights the static intent of the educational system from the 18th century through current practices, and offers a solution.

This "solution" or idea is proposed as an eclectic model of teaching that is responsive to the needs of the learner. This model encourages ownership of one's voice and draws on the strengths of our young people who have otherwise been outcast because of their differences. Poetry, as a content of instruction, is emphasized as it draws on these students' experiences, values, and voices. This shift from teacher–directed to student–driven instruction essentially levels the playing field for a fair education for all, despite perceived and real challenges.

I see instruction for those individuals who are at the mercy of the dominant culture (who refuse to accept and embrace them) from what I call a "therapeutic" point of view within a systematic and structured approach. This approach seems to engage the young people I've taught, bringing those who have chosen to alienate themselves attempts to bring them closer to the "fountain."

But before I present some of my ideas, let me review some of the major "themes" that I believe have most influenced education today: themes in education developed in response to major movements such as Christian theology, the Enlightenment, and Scientific Reductionism. Currently, technological problem–solving drives so–called critical thinking as a major component of our schools' curricula.

Unfortunately, like the marginalized youth with whom I have worked, it seems schools, too, are thirsty for a taste of "success." This may materialize in the form of a philosophy or a particular method and/or practice for teaching, or a single test expected to measure results and publicize a district's success. And therein lies the conflict: Is school about success for the individual or the success of the school district and the community as a whole?

It is dangerous to drink from only one ideological pool. Teachers need to have the opportunity to investigate and research a variety of skills, content ideas, and strategies that will benefit diverse learners, not just the society as status quo. Effective teachers know how to develop curriculum that is structured, yet still reflective and child–centered. It is in comparing the importance of program initiatives metaphorically—a single drop of water falling (versus the collective needs of our young people), spreading and reaching out, that one will gain insight. A ripple with so many lasting rings far outreaches the initial drop of a particular district mandate. Therefore, it is the learner we need to touch, as the district mandate does not function in society; people do. In order to understand how one achieves this, one must, I believe, understand the evolution of education.

The Evolution of Education

The structure and ideals of early Christian theology suppressed human possibility by embedding an element of human depravity into the belief system (Miller, 1990). Students learned to be devout followers. Protestantism delivered a clear message of "original sin" which was considered to be inborn and, thereby, inescapable. Therefore, discipline and memorization of the Bible were stressed in school as a means to living a pure life (Miller, 1990). However, there then became conflict between the pious worshippers in the church and those who were searching for greater knowledge of the natural world, leading to the rise of the Scientific Reductionism movement.

The "universal truths" of scientists such as Newton and Galileo provided this reinforcement. Suddenly, there was a broader understanding of the universe. This enabled individuals to shift the burden of original sin. Laws of planetary motion with the sun as the center of the universe and the suggestion that the earth moves were held in contempt by the church. Many people's belief systems, then, shifted toward impersonal laws. These laws were not impacted by reflective soul–searching and measures of human value. Education included more questioning and reasoning as people came to believe that they could have some measure of control in the world (Miller, 1990) and thus ensued a sense of control that continued to make them accountable to the common beliefs of the majority. So although there had been a change in thinking, there was still an emphasis on conformity to the community.

This belief prevailed as conservative leaders continued to stress obedience and discipline. In the United States, for example, Benjamin Franklin believed that humans, as individuals, were "ungovernable." He felt that people needed education in order to be members of the larger society. Franklin believed that man should conform in order to view themselves as "public property" (Miller, 1990, p. 20).

While accountability to one's religion may have waned, people were still very accountable to the society as a whole. The intent of education was still not reflective of the individual. The individual was to be shaped to the greater good of the community. This was achieved in an autocratic school system stressing such conformity. It was not until later, during the early 20th century, that there was any small transformation in the message conveyed by members of society. Even then, these individuals were in the minority. They included such liberal progressives as Jane Addams and John Dewey.

This period in time saw a movement toward a more humane and reflective philosophy of teaching. It included the establishment of settlement houses. These "shelters" offered individuals opportunities not only for social services, but for education and "literacy."

John Dewey supported this "unethical" style of teaching and learning—that is, one that stressed the individual's needs and abilities. He recognized Emerson's beliefs and practices on learning as he emphasized the genuine need for children to connect their lives' experiences to their classroom lives. This paralleled Emerson's references to non–conformity and spirituality. (Ironically, Emerson's spiritual declaration of independence became public two generations after our nation's political Declaration of Independence [Mumford, 1979.]) And yet, in reality, this did not lead to a transformation in education. The purpose never really changed. Education was still a means to establishing the social order.

Education became a "true" institution post–World War I. Standardized testing became a means for discrimination. Immigrants and war veterans became the "marginalized" population as they were passed over for powerful positions in their communities and workforces. The stratification of society and our school systems was effectively in place. The hierarchy of power had been systematically perpetuated. Scientific testing such as the Stanford–Binet IQ test was utilized to demonstrate the alleged superiority of the privileged, Anglo–Saxon male.

The Cold War reawakened the same old concept of conformity under a new title called "consensus consciousness" (Miller, 1990, p. 52). Everyone was expected to view the world in the same anti–communist manner. As industrialization took over the nation, spirituality waned. Capitalism and its economy, that is, the production of goods and services, began to drive society and its schools. Curricular decisions became more heavily influenced by standardized testing, which in turn determined the amount of State and Federal funding. Inquiry was not valued; the production of a product was.

Service and conformity were a reflection of the "purpose of education" from the beginning of the idea of public education in our country. This has been the ongoing conflict that ultimately has led politicians, administrators, teachers, and even families to seek out that "one" program that will turn the tide in learning. And, yet, even as the "conflict" remains intact in schools and in school curricula today, the "purpose of education" is still touted as a means to meet the needs of the larger society, to maintain the social order. Schools still perpetuate a class system that democracy claimed to absolve. Children continue to be sorted by privilege, wealth, gender, and the color of their skin. Society as a whole needs to be involved in a complete change in philosophy as to the purpose of education.

Educators should never be comfortable with viewing students as products. The intent should never be to come off the assembly line with a score in hand in order to receive dollars for such efficiency. This point is even more crucial in the face of increasing standards and a return to standardization.

I Am Still Thirsty: Solutions Based on "Voice" through Poetry

With this background in place, one can more thoroughly evaluate current programs and why they exist. The structure of society perpetuates the need for conformity at different levels. Therefore, many teachers implement programs supporting current district needs and dictates. While this may enable kids to achieve expected reading and writing scores on standardardized tests (although it often does not), the process of learning, as well as nurturing student voice, is often neglected (Cohen, Polloway, & Wallace, 1987). And students are not committed to these programs because they aren't able to share in the ownership of the teaching and learning.

This fact introduces a critical element in the education of children. Regardless of the programs and the strategies one implements, kids need to feel valued. A child simply will not and cannot learn until he or she has made an emotional connection with his or her own ideas about himself or herself. Only then will he or she connect with the world around them. As we have seen, society has traditionally tried to come before the individual and, hence, the alienation and marginalization of those who do not conform.

Years of being excluded from the public "fountain" leads individuals to "refuse" and to seek out a new pool from which to drink. Everyone, even the "multiply–marginalized" adolescents with whom I have worked, need water to survive. Water is survival.

In this next section, I will share how students, after years of marginalization, actually "excelled" in an environment that encouraged reflection and meaningful dialogue and found, at least temporarily, a collective fountain where they were all welcome.

Implementing Poetry in My Classroom

My research took place in my self–contained classroom for students with special needs, a classroom that included six pre–adolescent and adolescent students (ages 10 to 13), me, and a paraprofessional. In New York State, this setting is considered the "most restrictive" for students with special needs. Their family dynamic or academic histories necessitate the need for a highly structured setting in order to meet these students' needs effectively.

The population included students who were either labeled "learning disabled" or "emotionally disabled." The nature of this type of class, or an "Option III," was traditionally seen as a kind of "catch–all" setting for students with learning disabilities, a term defined by New York State (the definition varies state by state) as applying to those students who have "a 25 point discrepancy between their cognitive ability or I.Q. test scores and their actual achievement." For example, a fourth–grade student functioning at the second–grade level would qualify in New York State as "learning disabled." (Of course, there is much controversy around how these students' skills are measured, i.e., the kinds of assessment tools used by the state and the various school districts. Major confounding issues such as native language or English proficiency are often not even looked at carefully. Certainly a much fuller discussion is warranted; unfortunately, I cannot do that here.)

And yet, included in this same setting are students who have extreme emotional needs. These are children often with significant socio–emotional difficulties; all of my students lived in an urban area where they also faced many socio–cultural challenges such as discrimination, poverty, absence of role models, and lack of opportunities. In the Option III classroom, then, education plans include strategies that empathize "coping skills" and other ways to strengthen behavioral skills such as interaction with peers and the ability to verbalize or to express, in some way, needs or feelings. General intellectual functioning of these students is average to above–average according to formal assessments. Unfortunately, in my classroom, these students' academic performance (and behavior) did not reflect such strengths.

The situation was very difficult. One must meet the needs of kids who require academic strategies and compensatory strategies for visual, auditory, language, or processing weaknesses. In addition, one must address the emotional needs of students dealing with internal conflicts such as self–esteem, anger, depression, and feelings of worthlessness. The common link seemed to lie in structure and reinforcement of positive behaviors. Firm limits and consequences needed to be clearly articulated. This helps keep the students with learning disabilities on task while "managing" the behaviors of the students with emotional challenges.

With behaviors and strategies in place, however, it is time to address the curriculum needs of these students. They are not grouped by grade level, but rather by the severity of their disability. The standards for grade promotion are ambiguous at best. And yet, a New York State curriculum must be in place. For example, seventh–grade science materials must be modified to reflect the level of student achievement.

Reading and writing were the most challenging for my students. Consequently, these were the areas that required the most modification and the most attention. In fact, students with learning disabilities, were originally placed in remedial reading classes as a rule (similar to how many English language learners were placed in classes for students with disabilities). Some research, however, does estimate that more than 85% of all students with learning disabilities also have specific reading disabilities, which make their writing performance "dramatically different" than their non–disabled peers.

Primarily because of this dilemma, as well as observing my own students (who for the most part were tested at reading and writing levels of first to second grade), I, along with the help of Brett Blake (my professor of English as a Second Language [ESL] at the time) decided to pursue research associated with the writing needs of these very special adolescent students in my classroom.

Initial Efforts

The initial intent was to incorporate some sort of interactive element into my writing curriculum so that my kids would connect with "real" audiences and therefore feel more motivated to write. I introduced the theme of "International Pen Pals" as part of a writing unit, hoping to pair my students up with students in the former republics of the Soviet Union (I had found a packet of information on doing this while conducting a school computer search in the school library).

While this holistic approach was well organized, it did not interest the students at all. The material was too vast and simply not connected to their own experiences. While maps, pictures, stories, and pen pals were provided with the kit, there was not enough experience to link the kids to the activity. They did write letters, but it required a lot of prompting and redirection. Word processing the letters on the computer was offered as an incentive for the students to complete their letters, and yet it was still not the "writing experience" the students were after. The completion of the task of writing a letter to a pen pal seemed to provide minimal opportunity for growth, so although it did satisfy the eighth–grade standardized testing format for letter writing, it did not satisfy either me or my students.

I didn't give up hope; however, after I had completed the entire unit on writing, I noticed that poetry had been, by far, the most productive, reflective, and dynamic piece of the unit for my students. I believe that there were two reasons for this: First, there is only a subtle emphasis on grammar, syntax, and semantics. (Reading and writing and using "correct" standard, white American English is such a tremendous obstacle for students like mine). Second, poetry related to these students' life experiences. Expression and experience are really the learners' most valued skills. Therefore, poetry meets the needs of these learning–disabled students struggling to achieve academic success while simultaneously helping the emotionally disabled students share part of themselves.

Teaching Poetry: Beginnings

In a society that increasingly questions the roles and responsibilities of teachers, I believe one needs to investigate what is truly valuable to the learner, especially a learner who has been traditionally denied access to what is considered "valuable" in society. Teachers' priorities should be shifting toward curriculum that is, thereby, responsive to the interests and strengths of their learners. And although the teaching style of poetry supports very traditional philosophies of education such as reflection and critical thinking, it also allows for less traditional ways of learning, such as expression of voice.

Unfortunately, the minds of people both in schools and in society have become mechanized and desensitized. Thoughtfulness and reflection are not virtues that are valued. Industry, capitalism, and materialism do not cultivate balance between the individual and society. In the current social order, objects and things are more significant than thoughts and feelings (Miller, 1990, chapter 2).

Poetry is a means to reawakening the thoughts and feelings that have been suppressed by the ever–swinging and changing pendulum that defines educations. But it requires a certain level of soul–searching.

Poetry has unique rhythm, meter, rhyme, or even an "off–rhyme" which conveys feeling and voice. Multi–sensory teaching provides students with the opportunity to engage in feelings and sounds as a means to learning. It evokes experience beyond basic reading and grammar and taps strengths that are suppressed during drill and practice lessons.

Poetry had been successful for the students I taught during the fall of that year. The profile of each student supported the need for a highly structured program with "rich" reinforcement. With those variables in place, the class generated vast amounts of poetry that reflected their personal styles and voices. And it was fun. Below are some samples from that initial period.

"The Talking Rock" was a poem written by a 12–year–old girl who, according to her records, "could not read nor write." This statement was supported by her standardized test scores, her academic history, and her behavior. Her Individual Education Plan (IEP) supported the need for a scribe to read and write for her. I believed she clearly had skills and abilities that were suppressed by socio–emotional issues and inappropriate behaviors. And yet, she wrote poetry.

The Talking Rock

I am looking at a Rock
It is a Happy or Sad Rock
It is a Rock that can talk
It will tell the story

But, I do not know
If it can talk
I would like my rock to talk to me
It will be a Happy Rock and I will love it.

Similar results were achieved for all six students. One young man, whom I'll call James, wrote the following:

Me
Restless Tired
Running Playing Hanging
Ball Book Hall Shoes
Rapping Shopping Reading
Big Bad
Me

James, usually apathetic and uncaring about school, had a school history that would explain why: James repeated the first grade and was subsequently "socially promoted" onto the fourth and fifth grades where he was then labeled "learning disabled." At this point, it was noted that his reading level was equivalent to that of a preschooler who was at a "reading–

readiness" stage. In general, James had poor self–control, didn't like to follow rules, and had trouble paying attention. With poetry, I believe, he was transformed.

The students' expression, voice, and their ability to produce written material (especially considering that many of their IEPs stated they simply could not read or write) gave significance and meaning to this unit for me as their teacher. They shared an element of their character as caring human beings—similar to Noddings' (1999) "circles of caring", a philosophy that says that students who care for and value themselves (and I say, those who are given these opportunities) are able to adapt and more genuinely care for other people and things in society. Noddings elaborates:

> Students have pressing cares and interests not addressed by the subject matter presented in schools. These are the issues and insights we, as educators, have a responsibility to explore from the learners' point of view. The child–centered approach of listening to the student should be a priority over the systematic goal of control: the goal of the state to control content, the goal of administrators to control teachers and the goal of teachers to control kids. (p. 9)

In retrospect, then, I had learned that while the pen pal component of the writing unit did not work, poetry seemed to bring my students alive, and I was therefore eager to try it out again the following year.

There were three new students in my group the following year, again totaling six: A 12-year-old reading and writing at a K–1 level, three achieving at a second–grade level, and the remaining two other learners consistent with a fifth–grade level of reading and writing. The most common challenge these students exhibited was frustration and self–doubt (especially regarding the idea that they had anything interesting to say). They were embarrassed to write and often acted out to disguise their weaknesses. Despite some initial denial of "I don't do poetry," however, each student wrote (some prolifically); and the unit was a success.

The material generated was thoughtful and reflective of student interests. The strategies for teaching included walks outside for "Haiku, a poem about nature"; sculpting nouns for "Diamante," a poem subtly incorporating the conventions of grammar; and baking cookies for our "Shape" poem, poems that use descriptive words to fill in the shape of an object.

Each student had his or her own unique interpretation of the unit. They enjoyed the free–flowing poems where they thought they could be most expressive and, also, I thought, most sad, frightening, and honest.

The following poem, "The Crazy Woman," was written by a young man who was being raised solely by his aunt. His mother had died when he was an infant and he had been raised by his grandmother until she recently died. His aunt was doing the best she could to provide the love and guidance he needed—but who is this "crazy woman"?

The Crazy Woman

He is frightened
He is scared of his own mother
She is very ugly and crazy
He hears not a sound
Because he is deaf
This is all a dream

Another young man who had lived through a very violent family history (he saw his brother being shot, his cousin was found murdered, and his uncle was missing and presumed dead) shared also his most frightening honest thoughts through poetry:

Pink little woman
Pink little woman
Dressed in Black
Smacked the Children
On their backs
Killed one child
and
Went to Hell
Pink little Woman
Pink little Woman

Noddings' (1999) "cycle of caring" includes "reception, recognition, and response" (p. 15) to emotions. This must be modeled, discussed, and practiced for learners to generalize the concept. Poetry is a fine way to initiate the "cycle." It is a curriculum that allows for expression of honesty while avoiding the controls of standard paragraph writing. Poetry is anything but the current standardized liberal arts education.

Maybe we shouldn't judge kids by one human capacity that can be measured and tested. Maybe the ability to synthesize data from two documents isn't how we should determine the value or worth of kids. Maybe computation of problem–solving measures ensures inequality for all. Is that why we continue to sort kids by arbitrary skills...because it perpetuates our history of separation, segregation, and rejection?

The ideas shared by these students support their need and desire to communicate, to be heard. They do not respond well (at all!) to worksheets and spelling quizzes. They need the opportunity to trust, to care, and to share. That is the role of our schools. Society will not change. Therefore, we teachers need to become more transformative in our roles as educators. I know that once students achieve the basics of self–worth and value, they too will come to the well to drink. To drink and to achieve.

Implications from Stephanie's Story

Stephanie's Option III classroom was yet another place where the culture of refusal had taken hold: a space where students' frustration was as acute as the others whose lives we have read about in previous chapters—acute as they resisted (and consequently are "refused") on multiple levels. The first level, of course, is the placement these students have received into a "special needs" classroom. The second results from the first: these students are doubly–segregated by their placement and by other socio–cultural factors such as the color of their skin, the language they speak at home, or the poverty they endure. But there are also not–so–obvious factors at play. These students' disabilities have taken center stage and therefore have become the resistance (both by the students and often the teachers) itself. That is, Stephanie's students (and certainly others like them) create and ultimately fulfill a self–fulfilling prophecy: "troubled," "defiant," unable to "control" their behaviors (including, of course, their refusal of schooled literacy); in many ways, they are excused from any real attempts at being educated. They are deemed "unreachable" and "incapable" because the challenges and hurdles are simply too much for (some) teachers, administrators, and communities to overcome.

But Stephanie took her students' resistance as a challenge and worked hard to design curricula that could showcase her students' capabilities that she knew were there. And indeed, through her hard work, first through a not–so–successful unit on pen pal writing and then by a very successful unit on poetry writing, Stephanie, at least temporarily, felt that the culture had been punctured; that she had actually led them to the well.

Remember the young man's poem about the crazy woman. Here, we saw a frightened, resentful, and reflective piece that revealed the pain he had endured as a result of living his life without his mother and, more recently, his grandmother. This poem revealed the agony that this adolescent lived with, perhaps on a daily basis: an agony that undoubtedly contributed to his "emotional challenges." Look, too, to the poem by the student who writes of "Me." As he attempts to create and carve out a self–identity, he plays with many feelings…"restless…tired…big…bad." For the first time since she had had him as a student, Stephanie reported that affording this adolescent the opportunity to talk about himself gave him a real sense of control about his life—a sense of control that one might hope would carry over into his "disability" of having little self–control.

Interestingly, this is where it all begins and ends: in the classroom. This is where the culture of refusal's seed is planted—where it grows, and is nurtured, blossoming into an all–powerful, encompassing disability. As we re–think the stories we have read of the incarcerated and migrant adolescents, we realize that, even for those who weren't labeled to have special needs, (and far too many of them were) schooling looked much the same. In other words, there were few, if any, teachers; few in any curricular materials; and few if any support systems from these students' schools, families, or communities that worked to include them. So as Fine (1991b) reminds us, "dropping out of…school can be analyzed as an act that reflects in some cases a student's articulated politic of resistance" (p. 396). In the case of Stephanie's students, perhaps, it is their only politic of resistance.

Millions of dollars are spent on "special education" across the country, and it has been reported that that figure is only on the rise. Particularly disturbing, however, is the fact that the preponderance of special needs students are African–Americans, especially young boys and men who live in urban areas, are poor, and who may speak a language other than English. Why are so many of these young men labeled as such? And why, as Stephanie suspects (and has heard anecdotally from fellow teachers and administrators) do these students, in particular, dropout and end up in jail? And, of course, where are the teachers who can stop this? Why, as Stephanie reminds us, aren't there more teachers willing to become "transformative" in a quest to bring all students "to the fountain to drink"?

I will discuss some of the possibilities of Stephanie's work in the final chapter of this book; but first we again meet Colleen, this time in her role as an adult education teacher of migrant workers, teaching late at night in the camps and the cinder block barracks where her students lived and worked. Her story, too, provokes much thought, reflection, and questions as we try to come closer to answers to guide us in teaching and learning with "multiply–marginalized" adolescents in our schools today.

Chapter Nine

Teacher Literacies: Colleen's Migrant Labor Camp Classroom

And the world
is less bitter to me
because you will retell the story.
(Boland, 1994, p.50)

As a child growing up in a college town, I had the luxury of going to the university laboratory school from third to sixth grades. However, somewhere in the middle of my stay there, the university (and later the federal government) decided to integrate our elite world with the children of migrant workers, and later city kids, who were bused in, much to the horror of many of the townspeople (and I'm sure some of the so–called progressive academics whose children attended the lab school). But, before I got to know any of these students, like countless other white students, I was transferred out of the lab school to the local public school at the end of sixth grade. My only memories of the migrant kids was that they were quiet, and of the city kids, that they were loud. But I never thought much again about either population over the years until Colleen became a student in my graduate ESL methods course.

About Colleen
Colleen enrolled in graduate school many years after she received her bachelor's degree. She had taken time off, like many of my female students, to get married and raise a family. Colleen was always very active in the community and in her daughters' schools, but as her children grew, she did, too, realizing (like many of us do) that the world was far from the just place we had hoped, and believed, it was. Going back to school was a logical step toward being "more of an activist," she once told me.

Colleen made many sacrifices to return to school, including less time with her children and less money. Just getting to graduate school, for example, took her an hour and a half each way, in good weather. And when the "snow belt" on which she lived became true to its name, blanketing the entire region in literally feet of snow, blowing spume off the Great Lake that caused "white–out" conditions, it could take Colleen double that amount of time. But she came anyway. And like Stephanie, she became a graduate assistant in the ESL program, studying her teaching and her students and thinking deeply about why she was teaching and what teaching meant. She, like Stephanie, also asked a lot of questions and inspired me in ways sometimes I only now begin to understand. Here is her story.

Colleen's Story

I nervously raised my hand. I was a student in Brett's Graduate ESL methods course, and hesitant about the question I was going to ask.

"Ok, Brett. Maybe I shouldn't even ask this. It'll sound stupid. But here goes. Why would these guys *want* to journal anyway? Don't they just have to learn how to *speak* English? I mean, if they're working all day on a farm, what use would journaling be to them anyway? And besides, what would they ever use it for?"

I had been teaching ESL at that time for about six months, using mostly workbooks provided to me by the adult education program for which I worked. As I followed along with the books, little did I realize then how my techniques would drastically change over the next few years.

"Try it," Brett said. "Your students have a lot to say. Journaling will allow them to express what is in their hearts. What's inside there will lead to use of authentic language experiences in your classroom. Give them a chance. Let them lead *you*."

At that time, I was teaching at a migrant labor camp in rural western New York State. The migrants' housing consisted of a row of barrack–style rooms off a rural country road. I had a steady group of 10 to 12 students, ranging from 13–year–old Jose, spending his first summer working in the United States to Paulo, who, from his weather–beaten features, looked to be in his late 50s or early 60s.

Our class met in the kitchen of the camp, the center room in the row. The kitchen consisted of two picnic tables, two stoves, a refrigerator, and a sink. At the end of the kitchen was a little area that looked like a closet. This was the shower area. Such was our classroom.

The class officially met at seven p.m. At least that's when I would come for class. In the late summer, especially, students would arrive in ones and twos, each class beginning progressively later and later, depending on the weather or how late the sun would set. Sometimes class didn't really get rolling until about eight or eight–thirty.

Students might duck in, say a quick hello, then go to their rooms and gather up their personal items, and get in line for their turn in the shower room. This line might consist of six to eight workers waiting for a shower, or even to bathe their little ones. At the other end of the room stood five or six men, and maybe one or two women either cooking or making tortillas by hand.

Well, I hesitantly thought, what have I got to lose? So, I went to a drugstore the next morning and bought about 20 two–pocket folders, the kind with metal tabs, for inserting loose–leaf paper. Into each folder, I inserted 20 or so sheets of paper (low budget journals). I took the journals and some pencils to class the next day, and after a few students were gathered at the table and I handed them out, here is how one student reacted:

> Paciano: What do we do with these, miss?
> Coleen: They're journals. They're yours to keep. We'll use them in class for you to write in.
> Paciano: Miss, I don't know how to write in English.
> Collen: Don't worry. Write in Spanish, if you want. Write in English if you know the words. Even if you don't know the word, write down what you think it sounds like. We'll worry about the spelling later.
> Paciano: What do we write, miss?
> Collen: Anything you want. Or, if you're really stuck, I can give you some ideas to start off.
> Paciano: Miss, I don't have anything to say.

So began our experiment with journal writing, me and a group of students who've never been asked what their dreams, hopes, or aspirations were, let alone to chronicle them! Young men and women. Guys whose very lives and experiences literally have been pushed off to the edges of our little town. Ask most of my neighbors, and they wouldn't be able to tell you that a migrant camp is hidden in the woods only two miles from our middle–class–Main Street–neat row of homes. I wasn't much more aware. I, the teacher of migrant workers, who didn't think that they had much to say. Was I in for a surprise! (Please note: Throughout this chapter, I present my students' writings without correction except where meaning would be lost. After many of the student selections, I present my written thoughts—a kind of internal dialogue that I used to reflect on the transformations both my students and I were experiencing. To distinguish the two, I identify each writing or thought with the author's name, including my own, where appropriate.)

> Sometimes I like to be some places I dream like Because the dreams are beautiful and there the most Because when you dream it makes you think about it all the time and you be thinking (Antonio, Age 16).

> Wow, I thought. Dreams. He's got dreams. And I hadn't ever asked about them. This teacher (me) needed to change her approaches in the classroom, and her ideas about her students. (Colleen).

This chapter will chronicle some of the changes.

Revelations

The following night was graduate school again. Time to share this revelation with Brett and the class. We agreed that I needed to know more about my students. If I were going to be an effective teacher, the "one–size–fits–all" workbooks would have to be shoved into a corner. Reading, writing, listening, and speaking in our classroom needed to have meaning and value in *their* lives, instead of focusing on my conception of what they needed to learn.

Antonio's parents have been spending the harvest season in the United States for the past five years. For the past few summers, he had been attending the local migrant summer school. But now that he was older, he and his parents decided that he could spend his summers working. His education over the past few years had been split between schools in New York and Texas. A few winter months were also spent in Mexico, when his parents were unable to find work in either Texas or New York.

The word among the teachers in his district was that this student was just plain trouble. He constantly disrupted the classroom, and taught the other kids to swear in Spanish. He wouldn't do anything they wanted him to do. Maybe they hadn't asked him about his dreams either.

> I don't really remember any teacher that I had so far Because I forget a lot of the teachers that I had the First time. So I kind of remember is the teacher is Hilda. She was so bad she hit me with my fingers up and with the eraser it hit the tip of my fingers (Antonio, Age 16).

Maybe I wasn't doing that kind of physical damage. But, discounting students' experiences probably was stunting them just as much. I had so much to learn about who my students were and what was important to them. Slowly they became comfortable writing in their journals, sharing what was in their hearts and minds (Colleen).

> My life is not fine because I missed my family and my brother. Here in the united states [sic] I'm not feel well. Sometime I feel sad because I missed them I could see them very soon and I will be happy. Sometime I'm thinking about my girl-friend because I loved her sometimes she told me Leobardo you will be mine for-ever. And I say if you loved me prove to me and so she kissed me.

Today I feeling very well to see my girlfriend she is nice and very, very thin but love her so much. She told me that I'm beautiful. I think my girlfriend she is crazy but I'm not sure (Leobardo, age 18).

This entry was particularly stunning to me. A smack on the side of my head. This was what Brett was talking about. Authentic writing, from deep inside my students. Finally, I was listening. I began seeing Leobardo as a young man with deep emotions. I wanted to give him the opportunity to express them on paper whenever he felt the urge to write. Leobardo began to take another journal with him to work and on little trips with his family. He showed this one to me in class one day, but didn't offer me a chance to read it. Pages and pages, written by a young man whose teacher hadn't thought would have any use for writing at all (Colleen).

Students also began to talk about the losses they had experienced as they moved from one state to another. In the following entry, Roberto writes about leaving his friends and family in Mexico. According to his transcript at school, he had only gotten enough credits toward graduation to qualify him as a freshman. (After doing some more checking around, I found that he was characterized by teachers at school as a kid who would "sit in the back of the room, wouldn't interact with other students, and refused to participate.") I wondered what was going on in his head. His journals began to show me. Roberto had only completed five years of school in Mexico. Then, he had spent the remaining years of his education traveling back and forth between Texas and New York. He was not very fluent in either language. Here, Roberto writes emotionally about his memories of leaving his much–loved family. (As with the students' English, I have chosen to leave their Spanish misspellings intact).

Quando youme despedi cuando venia para n y me despedi de mi primo y vi como yoro porque nos queria mucho y mi tio bebita tambien y mi tia ade. Y mi amigo de el tambien me despedi y fue mal como verlos yorar mis amigos yo no me despedi de ellos que mal pero no para que algunos yoraran no major no en mexico bibia vein no se porque nos venimos fue muy mal para desperdirme mis amigos y mi familia. (When I left when I came to New York when I left, I saw my uncle crying, becasue he loved us very much, and my little uncle, too, and my Aunt Ade. And my friend also, I left him, and I felt bad to see my friends cry and I didn't want to leave them bad because some of them were crying and nothing in Mexico was good because I didn't know why we were coming and had to leave my friends and my family) (Roberto, age 19).

Roberto and Antonio are examples of two students for whom the "classic" model of education—schooled literacy as Brett calls it—had failed. They carried with them walls of protection—cultures of refusal—built and re–built every time they began a new school year. Here in our makeshift classroom, these students had begun to open up, to let down those walls. There was something about being on "their turf" that allowed them to feel comfortable enough to open up to me. I needed to figure out how I could keep those walls down when some of us went back to our "regular" classrooms at school.

The New School Year

The harvest season came to an end. Response journals had indeed helped keep the students' walls down. I had made what I considered to be pretty good connections with my students. They had opened up once I started listening to their voices. But I had much more to learn.

The school year began with my usual mix of Mexican students, some migrant and some settled. A rather homogenous group, all from the same country, same language, same race and cultural background. Our own little microcosm of what happens in a "mainstream" school. We were one. But this year someone "other" was added to that group. Someone from a different language background and an entirely different continent, and certainly from a different set of experiences than our little group. She even looked different from the rest of the students. They were mostly brown skinned, while her skin was as black as coal. The Mexican girls in the class wore ponytails. She had a head full of 18–inch braids.

She was the angriest, stoniest 15 year–old I had ever met. Her name was Esther, and she was from Africa. During the last few years, she had spent time in and out of refugee camps, depending on the intensity of the fighting in her country. Esther spent a year living in Philadelphia with her mother, had received Ds and Fs in her ESL classes, and was now living with her aunt and uncle in our rural town.

> I want to go back to Philly. I will tell my uncle that I want to go back to my mom if my mom doesn't want me to stay with her I will stay with my other uncle his name is Steve he is very nice to me. I don't want to stay here so my uncle children can be talkin to me every day if they do not want me [to] stay with their mom and dad. I will go back to philly that what I have on my mind today (Esther, age 15, first entry).

Weeks went by. Esther and the other students clashed. She and I clashed. She would come into our classroom, slam her backpack down on the desk, turn to me and with anger in her eyes and voice say, "I hate this class. I hate these kids. I hate this school." Ugh! A student in my class, hating it? Other teachers had come into my room in the past and told me that there was always a warm, homey feeling there. This was like a knife in my heart. I had allowed to happen the same thing that happened to migrant kids all the time. Feeling like an outsider; the other. Out of place. Apart (Colleen).

> I know how it feels when you have a best friend. When I was in Africa I use to hung out with a group of kids when I was living with my father after I when to school that morning I saw my father he came to my class. And when to my teacher can I speaker to Esther for a second. My teacher said Esther come up here. I ask my Dad, am I in trouble, he said no honey you are not in anything with me he said that your mom want you to come to her in America. I ask him when she want me come he [said] next week. I was all mad, he said why are you mad. I told him because you did not tell me on time now my friends are going to be angry at me. After my dad left I went to my friend and tell them that my dad want me to go to mom they all feel bad (Esther, age 15, composition draft).

During all of the angry, back–and–forth conflict with Esther, I hadn't stopped to consider where this girl was coming from, what all the problems were really about. I was just adding to them. I decided that it was time for me to start listening to Esther, and the voice within her.

Many of Esther's journal entries from then on began this way: "Dear Miss, How are you? I hope that you are fine through the grace of our Lord Jesus Christ." These entries and some stories that Esther began to share in class indicated just how important her faith and her church was to her. I decided that I would do a "modified" home visit, attending a Sunday service with Esther and her family. It took a couple of requests to get the schedule for the service. Esther was skeptical. She couldn't quite believe that her teacher was actually going to spend Sunday morning with her. I couldn't blame her. She and I didn't exactly have a peaceful relationship. Mostly, still, any time I took extra time with her was to reprimand her for something she was doing to bother the other kids in the classroom.

The church service was uneventful, but what was unusual was the smiles that came from down at the other end of the pew, where Esther kept leaning forward to look and see if I were still there. The stoney girl and her "reactionary" teacher spent the morning grinning at each other. After church, I met with her aunt to discuss Esther's progress in school, and Esther proudly shared with my friend and me stories of her tribe in Africa. It was a turning point in our student–teacher relationship.

By the end of that year, I was calling Esther our "miracle girl." She had slowly but steadily begun to trust me and the other students in our room. After I let my guard down and began to meet her where she was, to see her as a person, Esther let her own guard down. She shared herself in her writing, and through her love of music and poetry. She cheered on the most timid and reluctant students to participate and share, and became a well–loved member of the class. I believe that this happened because I finally stopped to listen to her voice—what was important to her.

New Directions in the Migrant Camp

The following summer, back in the camps, our class expanded our use of journaling. This time we included reader response in our work. My students had so much to say in their writing—why not see what literature could teach me about them?

I came to camp one night with a box full of children's literature—short books that the students could tackle in one night and then use to journal about before our next class. Most of these students had never had their own books, let alone been asked to write a response about them. I came to believe that these students had so much to tell me and each other.

Paciano, having returned to our little town for another summer of harvesting apples, eagerly chose Tomie DiPaolo's book, *First, One Foot, Then the Other*. In this story a little boy has a chance to help his grandfather learn to walk again, following a stroke.

> The grandfather is learn. The boy teach him. I like the book because I am learn too. I am learn my brothers. My brothers go to school. I want my brothers go to school. My brother younger he go school North Carolina. I want finish school and be how you say proud (Paciano, age 19).

Without this writing, I wouldn't have known that Paciano was just short of completing high school in Mexico, when he had to leave to support his nine brothers and sisters. I hooked him up with a teacher who taught GED en Espanol, and Paciano passed the exam the following summer. A few months ago, I ran into one of his cousins, who said that Paciano's family was now settled in North Carolina, and his younger brothers were doing well in high school, fulfilling Paciano's dream for them.

The moments of enlightenment for me occurred over and over. After I stopped thinking of my students as people with limits and instead as students who had so much to express and to share, the writing became more and more prolific. All from students for whom I questioned the very *need* to write.

Endings

Each night for the last 15 minutes of class last August, I read a portion of Gary Paulsen's *The Crossing* to my students. The students, exhausted from a day of working in the fields, would sit attentively listening to a tale so similar to many of their stories. In this book, the main character, Manny, a 14–year–old boy, plans to cross the border between Mexico and the United States, to escape the poverty and perils of life as a street dweller in Juarez and find work.

Josefino found in this book a story that stirred up so many memories of his own crossing. In his journal, through successive nights, he shared how he and his family crossed the border into the United States; how, as a 16–year–old, he was scared and forced to travel 10 hours on foot before they could meet up with a friend who had a van that would take them on the rest of their journey. The following is a passage from his response journal:

> I remember a family in Texas. They were Indians. I always remember them be-
> cause they helped us when our van was broke. I remember that they gave us Dr.
> Pepper. They were so nice to us. We had no money to give to them for helping us.
> They had some fields planted we stayed for some days to help them with the
> fields. We wanted to do something for them they helped us very much. I will al-
> ways remember these people. Some day, I want to go back to this place and find
> this family. To talk to them and see if they remember (Josefino, age 21).

Josefino will graduate from high school this coming June. He has not let the fact that he is older than other students get in the way of his dreams. He found his voice on paper, thought of himself as a student, and set himself upon a course of action to fulfill his dream of being the first in his family to get a diploma.

Paciano, Leobardo, Esther, and Josefino were my teachers. They taught me a lesson that I so very much needed to learn: that these "multiply–marginalized" students had a voice and I needed to value it. These students' very physical existence is hidden away from the "mainstream." Their homes are back away from the main road, where our town can keep them silent, and be silent about them. This injustice can keep students turned inward and incapable of even hearing their own voices ringing true: voices that speak of love and beauty and friendship and loss; goals and dreams. Voices that when finally heard by a willing listener can allow students to envision themselves as persons of value and worth.

Implications from Colleen's Story

Contrary to Stephanie's students, millions of dollars were *not* spent on helping to educate Colleen's students. In fact, the opposite might be said: little if any money was set aside in state or district budgets for these students. Their education was dependent on the good–heartedness of volunteers or people like the director of the summer migrant program, who continued to renew the federal grant (over 20 years) that provided the resources to pay teachers (like Colleen) to work with these students. Not surprisingly, the pay for teachers of migrant students is abysmally low. Most states are anxious to make the requisite funding available to provide for students with special needs because, in their constituents' eyes, to do so is admirable, even humane. But undocumented migrant workers are often living and working in the United States as "aliens," and as such state governments are far less inclined to allocate money for these "illegals." Yet, contrary to what seemed to have been the prevailing public opinion in 1982 (and today), the Supreme Court specifically ruled in Plyler v. Doe (475 U.S. 202 [1982] that:

> undocumented children and young adults have the same right to attend public primary and secondary schools as do U.S. citizens and permanent residents. Like other children, undocumented students are required under state laws to attend school until they reach a legally mandated age (School Opening Alert, 1998).

This Supreme Court ruling, therefore, while not giving additional or "special" funding or monies for migrant students, does implicitly state that the (read: any) funding available for general education in the *public* schools not be denied them.

Regardless of how much or how little was allocated and spent on helping to educate Stephanie's and Colleen's students, one thing remains clear: both groups of students remained outside the sphere of mainstream culture and of mainstream schooling. They either implicitly or explicitly resisted schooled literacy, and in turn were refused by the schools that so heartily perpetuated, and even defended, the values of the mainstream society.

Colleen, like Stephanie, understood the devastating effects this refusal had had on her students (remember the initial resistance when she brought journals to class that they could write or even had anything to write about) and had still persisted. By tapping into their local literacies, Colleen worked to help break the students' culture of refusal that for so long had engulfed their beliefs and even the perceptions of themselves. Think of the poignant story that Josefino wrote of the perilous crossing from Mexico that he and his family made, and the wonderful people who helped them when they reached the United States, or the insightful response that Paciano made to DePaulo's book, *Now One Foot, Then the Other,* revealing his deep feelings for his own grandfather and family members. Arguably, these students may talk and write about issues that are common among most adolescents or young adults. But from their writing, from their local literacies, we learned the details of *their* lives and the central role that tral role that many of these details played in their lives, facts that are meaningful and valuable to these students. This is not a minor point. Virtually all of their lives, these students had conceptualized writing and schooled literacy as something that could not go beyond the classroom—as something that did not, and could not, include their voices and their experiences. Breaking the culture of refusal, if only for a moment, had given these students a sense that their personal stories had meaning in the larger world.

Chapter Ten

Teacher Inquiry, Standards, and Culturally-Responsive Teaching: Implications and Future Directions for the Culture of Refusal

Children raised with dignity have a better chance of acting dignified; children growing up in peace and tolerance will more likely be tolerant themselves. Perhaps two simple guidelines can help us: respect the human dignity of each child; repudiate violence as a means of resolving disputes, solving problems, or giving lessons (Ayers, 1997, p. 188).

This book has been about children—children in adolescent bodies—capable of abstract thought and sexual activity; children caught between fitting in and carving out one's own self–identity. But these children have not been met with dignity as they attempted to make the transition into adulthood, certainly not from within the very places one would expect: in their families, in their communities, and in their schools. And so, in a desperate search for a place to call their own, they have resisted, rejected, and refused the scraps of mainstream society that they were thrown, creating and retreating to a safe space called "the culture of refusal."

The culture of refusal operates on many levels and manifests itself in many ways. To summarize and reflect on just how this culture of refusal has worked among the adolescents I have written about here, let's first return to the questions I asked in Chapter 1 and then review, briefly, each chapter in light of those questions.

The questions are: What can these adolescents tell us about school and society? What can we learn about youth who develop their own forms of literacy and (perceived) success? How does the culture of refusal work among these youth? And what does this culture tell us about schools, about how to change schools, and about how to affect change throughout society?

In Chapter 2, through a blend of feminist theory and critical race theory, we learn how crucial an analysis of race, ethnicity, class, and gender is in exploring how society's and the adolescents' perceptions and assumptions are shaped. Because traditionally these perceptions have often only been framed from within (and against) the dominant standard, the voices of these adolescents have been recorded, perhaps analyzed and synthesized, recycled again and again and again, yet unheard. With the tools of critical race theory, however, the analysis of these adolescents' voices is suspended so that it is the voices that we hear: the adolescents' lives in their own words and in their own terms. Critical race theory revealed to us, too, the relative privilege from which many of us come, and how profoundly different, and thereby potentially polarized, our lives and experiences are from the very students we may be teaching.

Chapter 3, on the topic of adolescent culture, briefly summarizes some of the major theories on adolescence from the turn of the 20th century to today. We learn here that the "multiply–marginalized" adolescents Ayers so eloquently defines share precious little with so–called mainstream adolescents, except for puberty itself. That is, the biological fact of puberty (and the resultant physiological changes) is a developmental factor experienced by all children as they make the transition into adolescence. The term "adolescence," however, is essentially a social construct, designed and developed by society to fit its needs. And middle schools and junior high schools were designed to differentiate, isolate, and sort adolescents for future work. In theory, too, middle schools were designed to protect the students they served.

The major challenge is, however, that middle schools, while succeeding in isolating and sorting students, do little to protect the fragile psyche of adolescents as they are faced with countless struggles such as identity formation and sense of worth and value. As a matter of fact, many middle schools accomplish just the opposite, and rather than easing the incongruence and uncertainty adolescents feel in today's society, only add to their unsettledness. And of course, additionally, and inextricably intertwined with adolescents' development and growth, are the socio–cultural contexts from which all adolescents are defined and perceived: Black, White, rich, poor, male, female, immigrant, transient, English–language–learning, educable, valuable—definitions that, exacerbated by institutionalized racism only add to the loss and despair many "multiply–marginalized" adolescents feel, especially in school.

In Chapter 4, I review the historical roots of our beliefs about literacy: about what constitutes "good" literacy; how power is associated with literacy, and how "good" literacy in the form of "schooled" literacy is perpetuated by society at the expense of the "local" literacies of countless communities considered outside the mainstream. It is here that we begin to get a sense, I believe, of the incredible loss we and our students may experience because whole groups of stories and texts are not deemed worthy enough to be discussed or read in schools. And it is here that I hope we begin to understand the potential contribution that the many and varied literacies (of multiple communities) may have on our abilities as educators to teach and to learn far beyond the traditional Western canon, potentially enriching our lives in ways we may have never thought possible.

Chapters 5 and 6 describe the settings (in which particular multiply–marginalized adolescents are expected to learn to become part of a mainstream) that do not value the kinds of experiences, the kinds of voices, and certainly the kinds of literacies these kids share. In Chapter 5, however, we read of a migrant summer school program that has been set up to counter the effects of these kids' "traditional" schooling as its teachers and staff worked toward including the migrant students' lives and experiences into the curriculum. Sadly, however, by the time many of the adolescents reached the age–equivalent of middle school/junior high, they were so jaded, all they wanted to do was to make money working in the fields alongside their families and friends.

The jail setting provided another glimpse into the kinds of "educational opportunities" poor, Black, non–native–English– speaking adolescents in this country can expect. Here, the students were not so lucky to have the backing of the institution itself. Rather, it seemed that only one or two teachers gave the adolescents opportunities to express their voices and connect their lives with the curriculum; others in the jail simply saw them as uneducable. Education was a privilege: a "rehabilitation" that only served (and was served by) those who played the game, followed the rules, and learned a particular brand of schooled literacy.

Chapter 7 highlights the adolescents' stories in their own voices and on their own terms. It is here that the migrant and jail kids write and talk about who they are, who they hope to be, and how they hope to get there. We hear clearly the pain, the frustration, the sorrow, the hope, and the joy of kids who are just that: kids. We learn the true nature, I believe, of their pain and how, then, this pain has led to quiet despair in some, to rebellious and violent reaction in others, and to a deep sadness for all. I believe that this is also the place that is, within the words of the chapter itself that we as educators begin to feel more strongly, perhaps, a certain sense of obligation toward fulfilling our mission as teachers who teach *all* children in equitable, and just ways.

And, finally, in Chapters 8 and 9, we read about two teachers who worked consciously (and tirelessly) toward breaking the culture of refusal among their students, bringing their voices to the center of the classroom: working, sharing, and helping these multiply–marginalized students to, perhaps, just for a moment appreciate who they are.

In the next section, I turn toward a discussion of the very real effects, and the implications of these effects, that a culture of refusal has had not only on these students, but also on education and society as a whole. Through this exploration, then, I discuss possible future directions. These directions include culturally-responsive teaching, curriculum, institutional, and policy change (e.g., standards, new certifications, and retraining). But more importantly perhaps, these next few pages help us gather ideas on how, as teachers and teacher educators, to bring a sense of awareness and understanding to our classrooms in a world that is, certainly at this moment in time, sorely lacking in compassion and mutual respect.

The Loss of Girls' Voices

As I discussed in Chapter 3 on adolescent culture, feminist researchers believe that at the onset of adolescence, most girls begin to separate formal educational experiences from other more personally meaningful experiences as they change, or modulate, their voices to better fit into society. For example, they watch what they say out loud, they monitor the kinds of opinions they have, and they often become mute in classrooms where earlier in their school careers they were fully–participating members. That is, adolescent girls learn and internalize the image of the "good girl" so well that they may alternately appropriate others' voices (saying what they think others want to hear) or silence their voices altogether. In previous research I carried out with pre–adolescent girls in an urban school in Chicago (Blake, 1997), I learned about the very real effects the loss of girls' voices had on a particular group of marginalized female adolescents. Yet it also became very clear to me the impact this kind of loss had on all girls, and hence, on society as a whole.

Promoting the notion of voice as providing both "public" and "private" spaces where girls can be alternately "engaged" and "resistant" as they express their most deeply–held feelings is a good one. But the lens of voice that affords girls opportunities in which to speak and write about their lives and literacies also puts them at a great disadvantage: not only were the Chicago girls' stories of domesticity and sexuality, for example, not valued in school because of the perceived essential nature of their stories as being strictly feminine; they were also rejected because these "girl" stories were not mainstream girl stories. (These adolescents wrote and talked about being the sole caretakers at night while parents worked, or of young friends of theirs having sex, or of the pervasive violence around them.) While mainstream girls learn (i.e., they are trained) to double their voices—one academic and male–like (they appropriate the voices necessary for schooled literacy)—these multiply–marginalized girls, on the other hand, do not. They maintain their resistant voices, engage in their own brand of a culture of refusal and, silenced, leave school altogether.

The adolescent girls in the migrant summer school classrooms spoke and wrote very much like the girls I worked with in Chicago and they, too, as we have seen, preferred to leave school and schooled literacy for the comfort and challenge of their families and their families' lifestyle as migrant farm workers. Their voices, too, expressed a sense of disengagement—a sense of resignation, as they, too, in Fine's (1991a) words, "are severed in their connection from schools by those schools they have a legal right to attend" (p. 3).

In this book, however, we have heard only the voices of adolescent girls in the migrant summer school. The female adolescents in the jail were not afforded the same privileges or rights as the male adolescents (remember, I was never "allowed" the opportunity to speak with the adolescent girls), and so even giving them the chance to engage in the schooled literacy opportunities offered to the boys were seen as inappropriate: the boys can't control their urges (when there were women about to walk the halls, a guard would yell, "Women on the floor," and all hallways were cleared of all male inmates); some of the girls had babies to care for; the girls were loud and spent their time complaining about everything they could. And so, too, in this controlled jail setting, where schooling was legally required (and provided for some), the girls suffered twice—a sort of double jeopardy—by virtue of their being female. The female adolescents in jail were doubly silenced, and thereby doubly punished, as they were not only physically held captive behind bars, but were also mentally held captive because of their gender. Their voices simply didn't exist.

The implications of not providing spaces in school, within schooled literacy practices, or by integrating girls' local literacies into the curriculum is enormous. Not only will the chasm between the "haves" and the "have nots" widen and deepen, but whole generations of girls like the ones we have read about here will resist, becoming part of the culture of refusal, where they will remain relegated to the sexualized and domestic roles traditionally held for them. These, I am told by the girls themselves, will be "dark and silent places"—spaces where they will live their lives in virtual anonymity.

And, yet, the implications are far–reaching for "mainstream" adolescent girls as well. In a culture that continues to degrade women as sexual objects; pays women less money for equal work than men; blames women for the breakdown of the traditional, nuclear family; blames female elementary teachers (elementary teachers are for the most part, women) for students' poor performance and behavior in school; and continues to relegate domestic and other feminine jobs to women, *all* female voices have the very real potential of going unheard. There is a saying, assumed to be coined by Paulo Freire (1986), the late writer, theorist, and revisionist who fought for equal education for all, that if one wants to know how well a society is doing, then one need only look toward its women as primary evidence. Granted, many societies do worse by its women; this society, however, has no excuse. Bringing all female voices back into the mainstream is not only wise policy; it is strong medicine.

The Loss of Boys' Hearts

It is fairly common knowledge today in the educational and psychological literature that girls lose their voices as they enter adolescence. It is not as typical, however, to understand that boys, as they enter adolescence and move through adulthood, lose their hearts. As I discussed in Chapter 3, there has been a resurgence both in the popular literature and in scholarly work, on this phenomenon. The "new psychology" of boys (Pollack, 1998) reveals that many boys entering adolescence today are "in real trouble" (p. xxiii). That is, they are twice as likely to be labeled as learning disabled, are 10 times more likely to be diagnosed with a serious emotional disorder, are being diagnosed with depression in ever–increasing rates, and are three times more likely to be the victim of a violent crime (other than sexual assault). Boys are forced to hide their true, inner feelings, and many feel desperately alone and afraid. In short, boys' hearts are being ripped from them, and replaced with a macho facade that most boys simply hide behind. Pollack (1998) elaborates:

> there is a major difference between the plight of boys and that of girls. Even when their voices are stifled in public, girls generally feel comfortable speaking in private to one another about their pain and insecurities. By contrast, though boys may exhibit bravado and braggadocio, they find it more difficult to express their genuine selves even in private, with friends and family. Their voices, as loud and forceful as they may sound, may not reveal what is really in their hearts and souls (pp. 13–14).

The hearts of the adolescent boys we have read about here have revealed this phenomenon as a reality—a painful reality that when intertwined with social class, lack of opportunity, and racism, has led these boys into situations of despair and hopelessness. To society in general, these multiply–marginalized boys appear to have no hearts at all.

Like the female adolescents in the jail, I have not provided as much information on the male adolescents in the summer school program. Whether because most of them were already working in the fields with their families, or because they were much more quiet with me (out of respect and cultural deference), we do, however, learn through their local literacies that they are resentful of a society that holds little opportunity for them. And yet, these boys also understood that they could (and did) return to their home countries at any time and, therefore, never felt, nor wished to feel, like full–time participating members in American society. The jail adolescents, on the other hand, felt their "Americanism" acutely, knowing full well that that was who they were and where they would remain, for better or for worse.

This loss of boys' hearts holds, too, enormous implications for society as a whole. Again, as the separation between the rich and the poor grows wider, there becomes an underclass of citizens that are deemed unreachable, undesirable, and uneducable. The strain (and drain) on our economic and political system will only grow heavier—if multiply–marginalized boys (and increasingly if "mainstream" adolescent boys) continue to swell the ranks of dropouts and fill the jails in unprecedented rates, society has, and will, pay a high price. The school shootings in white middle–class high schools around the country painfully reveal the extraction of this price: adolescent atrocities suffered by a society unable, and perhaps as of yet, unwilling, to explain its actions. The culture of refusal is there, potentially among all adolescent boys, manifesting itself in frighteningly similar ways.

Future Directions

In a poignantly written review of Anyon's latest book, *Ghetto Schooling* (1997), Sadovnik & Semel (2002) remind us that as we look toward the future in our quest to help multiply–marginalized students succeed, it is imperative that we view "educational reforms within the larger framework of the history, economics, politics, and sociology of education" (p. 28). In other words, "educational rearrangements" such as including local literacies into the curriculum and listening to students' voices are necessary, but not sufficient ways in which to ensure that multiply–marginalized students, too, are offered the "unlimited opportunities" in school that affluent, white children are offered. Sadovnik & Semel (2002) continue:

> [It is] a simplistic notion that school reform comes in neat packages under curricular and pedagogic rubrics, or that teachers and administrators, *alone* (my emphasis) can be agents of transformation in their schools…urban school reform is far more complex (p. 30).

Like Anyon (1997), Ayers (1997), Fine (1987, 1991a) and others, I believe that no reform can work (well) without addressing (and fighting against) the "insidious economic and social inequities" (Fine, 1991, p. 407) present in our society, and, hence in our schools, today. Simply changing school curricula (i.e., to include students' local literacies, for example) is not enough to bring these voices and hearts back into school and society. Indeed, so–called reforms such as increased standardization, strengthening the "back–to–basics" movement, and quietly pulling out of the curriculum any remnants of multiculturalism have been harmful and become:

> precisely the way to divert attention away from the unjust social and economic arrangements [that these adolescents experience], to further deform the process of education, and to guarantee a swelling of the ranks of [more] high school dropouts about whom we can then say, "If only…" (Fine, 1991, p. 407)

This is not to say, however, that reform should not begin (and continue) in the classroom among teachers and students. It should; it must—reform is absolutely crucial at the grassroots level—and it is here that many reform movements in education have actually begun (See Ayers, 1992, 2001, Kincheloe, 1991, 2001).

In the following section, I outline some ideas for future directions and further inquiry and research, both on the classroom, institutional, and policy levels.

What Can We Do as Teachers?

Our role as teachers is undoubtedly a complex one. Arguably, this role has become even more difficult as we are faced with a myriad of new policies (steeped in public opinion), new standards, greater accountability, and fewer resources. And yet our most compelling challenge comes from within our classrooms; from within ourselves and the students to whom we are entrusted with our knowledge. We as teachers need to begin to examine critically the cultural complexities that surround and infuse everything we teach. That is, we must interpret and reinterpret perspectives and assumptions around the diverse cultural knowledge and experiences that *all* children bring to school and, in doing so, find ways in which to extend these conversations into the curriculum (Schubert, 1986), particularly in our own classrooms with our own students.

Giroux (1988) elaborates:

> it is imperative for teachers to critically examine the cultural backgrounds and social formations out of which their students produce the categories they use to give meaning to the world. For teachers are not merely dealing with students who have individual interests, they are dealing primarily with individuals whose stories, memories, narratives, and readings of the world are inextricably related to

wider social and cultural formations and categories. [The issue] here is not merely one of relevance but one of power. (p. 177)

As we move toward an inclusion of all students' voices into the curriculum—into the schooled literacy practices of the classroom—only then can power be reconfigured and redistributed, resulting in the acknowledgement of, and the respect for, each other's diverse cultural knowledge and experience.

Culturally–Responsive Teaching

Both Colleen and Stephanie practiced what is often called "culturally-responsive teaching," using "culturally relevant pedagogy" (Ladson–Billings, 1994) which is often defined as one that is "specifically constructed in relation to the needs of children of color" (Sadovnik & Semel, 2002, p. 29). Culturally-responsive teaching in simplistic terms means that, as a teacher, one is responsive to the different cultures in the classroom and uses strategies and techniques that recognize each student's unique and diverse needs and learning styles. Simple enough? Perhaps. But culturally-responsive teaching also implies that the teacher finds compelling the "interwoven relationship among power, language and literacy that silences kids..." (Willis, 1995, p.39). She understands therefore the "richness" of her classroom as she attends to the "plurality and diversity" both within her classroom and throughout the United States and the world, and takes seriously the "historic past and the social and political contexts that have sustained it." The complexities of culture and all of its implications must take center stage in the classroom and hence in all the literacy practices and events in which the teacher engages the students.

Curricular Change: Literacy, Language, and Culture

Aside from attitudinal change, culturally-responsive teaching is reflected best through curricular change (Schubert, 1986). Literacy and language learning and development is reinterpreted and reflected in methods and strategies that not only acknowledge, but put forth the idea of active, engaged learning where meaning is constantly constructed and reconstructed through negotiation and interaction with others' and one's own historical, cultural, and social assumptions that shape and define schooling. Approaches such as process writing and a classroom–based reader response to literature espouse these perspectives. (Both Stephanie and Colleen engaged their students in strategies of both approaches. Refer to Chapters 8 and 9.

I have discussed in detail in Chapter 4 how a process approach to writing has helped many "multiply–marginalized" students to be able to express their local literacies, and in doing so, to experience some measure of "success" in their language and literacy development. A reader response approach to literature in the classroom also enables students to move their learning experiences and understandings to the forefront of their learning, and hence, too, their literacy development. (Specifically, in a classroom–based reader response approach to literature, the primary emphasis is on the student's oral or written response to text as the student creates his or her own meaning to the text, with the help of the teacher. Feelings, memories, associations, and intuition form the core of this classroom–based response to literature and students are validated and potentially enriched by sharing often similar responses with their peers and their teacher (adapted from Blake, 1996, p. 43).

Simply rethinking curricular choices, however, begs an analysis of broader issues and concerns—issues that Sadovnik & Semel (2002) remind us to think about very seriously:

> To what extent do low–income, children of color require a different curricular and pedagogical approach? Do African–American children need a special brand of pedagogic practice...Or are there best practices in teaching and learning that work for all children? Should they [schools] implement universal pedagogical practices for all children, regardless of race, class, gender, and ethnicity? Most importantly, is there empirical evidence on educational outcomes supporting either or both of these perspectives? (p. 29).

Indeed, in previous work (Blake, 1995, 1997), I have provided specific evidence that pedagogical practices that include all students' experiences and voices in the curriculum can be successful on an individual and classroom–based level. There is a bigger picture, however. This picture needs to help us focus on how we can restructure teacher education, the environments that produce "failing" schools, *and* a society that condemns those students whose lives, and hence their learning, has been defined by and within the larger historical, social, cultural, political, and economic forces at work.

What Can We Do as Teacher Educators?

In a course I taught at a previous university, I learned how crucial it was to talk with teachers about students who were potentially different than the white, middle–class, suburban pupils many of us take for granted as representing the "mainstream."

I had designed the course "Literacy and Culture" according to the new New York State requirements that mandate that all teachers be given more instruction in matters of diversity, no matter where they taught or what their previous experience had been. It was a course designed not only to introduce teachers to linguistic theory and cultural understandings, but also to review approaches and methodologies that may be more useful (or at least more sensitive to) these students' particular language and literacy needs. Out of a class of 40, at least 35 students resisted the idea that diversity even existed; and I learned how naive I was to think that (most) pre–service and in–service teachers had grappled with the important issues that such a discussion, or course, might entail. As the course progressed, I increasingly heard statements like, "Culture means nothing to me." "I have no culture, Why should they?" as the teachers themselves revolted—forming a culture of refusal of their own—and steadfastly argued against doing the work required of them around issues of diversity and language and literacy development.

To me, this experience indicates how desperately this type of work is needed in teacher education; and, in fact, many programs around the country are rewriting existing curriculum to infuse discussions of diversity into their programs. In the alternative, other colleges of education (often prompted by the state) are mandating such training, both for teachers and teacher educators, through new, required courses for certification. These courses, like the one I taught, have as their main foci notions of culture or diversity.

Willis (1995) argues, too, for the "direct" teaching of issues of diversity. In an article that she writes as a teacher, teacher educator, and parent on the effects that schooled literacy had on her own son as an African–American, she learns of the "cultural accommodation" her son made on a daily basis to the teacher's expectations. Increasingly, as she not only watched her son resist schooled literacy but also, then, observed his desperate feelings of being misunderstood (when he attempted to construct meaning in contexts more relevant to his culture), Willis became extremely concerned about his need to continue to have to "culturally accommodate" to the teacher's assumptions and expectations. Calling the teacher's actions an "unintentional disregard for the cultural history, understanding, experiences, and voice of…[students]" (p. 32), Willis offers specific suggestions that she sees as needed in the coursework that teacher education programs offer so that teachers themselves can no longer say they didn't "intend" to ignore the needs of their diverse students. These programs, at minimum, should:

1. make explicit the relationship among culture, language, literacy, and power,

2. train teachers to use cultural information to support and nurture the literacy development of all the students who enter their classrooms,

3. [help teachers] to transform their thinking about the role of language and culture in literacy development,

4. [help teachers] to understand the dynamic role that culture plays in   language and literacy development in defining school literacy.

There is also needed reform in the area of adolescent education, and interestingly enough, states such as New York have taken the lead in re-designing and retraining teachers with a "7 to 12 Certification in Adolescent Education." Coupled with new courses on culture and diversity, classes designed to discuss the specific needs of adolescents are crucial in teacher education reform. This is especially important if we are to continue our struggle to move more teacher education programs away from a traditional mainstream perspective to one that better meets the challenges and promises of a culturally and linguistically diverse student population.

Curricular Change: The Developing Adolescent

Reform in the area of adolescent education has been as slow and tentative as any other. In New York State, for example, entire certification areas have just recently been rethought and restructured. Rather than continuing its emphasis on elementary and/or secondary education (effectively skipping the whole middle school experience), for example, New York State now offers a stand–alone certification, "Adolescence 7 to 12." To meet the requirements the State has put forth, schools of education have had to design numerous courses that focus more clearly and critically on this period of development. This means, too, that, courses in this area must look at adolescence among minority students, paralleling the research (see Chapter 3) that tells us that moving through adolescence for these students is a perilous journey, indeed.

In a course that I teach pre–service undergraduate students, the course description reads as follows:

> Interdisciplinary study of human learning, growth, and development focusing on the adolescent years. Study in [the] dynamics of cultural, sociological, psychological, and environmental influences; implications for assessment and for selec-

tion of appropriate strategies to address student characteristics and content–area standards. Appropriate field experience to integrate educational theory and practice (St. John's University Undergraduate Bulletin, 2001–2002).

In the class itself, we talk extensively about differing experiences and expectations among *all* adolescents, particularly as they may relate to the experience of urban adolescents who grow up in very much the same circumstances that I have described in this book. Because I teach at an urban university in New York, many of my students grew up in New York City and the surrounding boroughs, and they, too, bring stories to this class about what it means to be an adolescent outside of the "mainstream" adolescent upon which so much of school practices and school curricula are based and at which they are aimed.

John (all my students' names here are pseudonyms, much to their dismay!), a 20–year–old African–American from New York City, writes about his painful adolescence and his desire to help others like him experience adolescence in a different way:

> Just as many teens and pre–teens would join me in stating today, to consider the adolescent years to be the greatest experience of my life would be a falsehood. In actuality, I still consider them to be some of the most complex years...One of my main reasons for my desire to become an educator is in large part due to my educational experience as an adolescent. To be misunderstood was commonplace, not on my own accord I believed, but rather it was the incapacity of others that caused me to be misconstrued. I don't recall much of the educational components of my adolescence...[but I do] remember a feeling of indifference concerning my teachers...

And Ellen, 21, a Korean–American who came to this country not speaking English well, writes:

> All through junior high school, I did not feel that my teachers were there for me. First of all, my junior high teachers seemed to hate all their students and kids in general. I didn't think I could talk to *any* teacher about my problems...teachers tended to be more caring about their students in high school.

And finally, perhaps, the most poignant comes from Steven, a 27-year-old Gulf War veteran, outspoken, bright, passionate, a product of a White father and a Hispanic mother, as he would describe himself, who writes:

> The only thing I remember about my adolescence was that it was truly lonely. I had many teachers and most of them now I see had no business teaching. They were all horrible. Most of them thought I was so bright but did not encourage me at all. Instead they pointed out my flaws. I cannot remember a single teacher that

helped me. I actually despised teachers. The worst part of it all was that instead of helping me with my problems, like getting me into a foster home, they ignored my pleas and just passed me on to the next grade. I am not stupid and actually pride myself that I am a pretty smart guy. It wasn't until this past year when a priest came to our class and talked about resiliency in adolescents. It finally came to me that I am one of those people and no matter what, I can succeed. This is why I want to be a teacher. I want to help all the children. I want to help those so called "Outcasts" that are ignored so much in our school systems. Adolescence is so hard.

It's not surprising that when I asked these undergraduates (many of them fresh from the adolescent journey themselves) about how we could reform middle school education, they were quick to answer simply, thoughtfully, and kindly:

As a teacher I want to be a positive role model for my students, I want to have them in a comfortable environment, where we can relate to each other. Adolescence is a really tough time for kids and they don't always want the advice of adults. So being a teacher I would like to develop a common ground and mutual respect. I want to be involved with the kids and maybe make it little easier for them to pass through their adolescent stage. I feel at such a critical time it is important for these kids to have someone to lookup to who they trust and be inspired by. I have had teachers that seem very miserable and instead of helping you it seems though they want to hurt you. I would really like to develop methods that would help me achieve this goal with my students. (Mayra, age 20)

What Can We Do as Community Members?

In Chapter 3, I discuss the crucial importance of three factors—family, school, and community—in working together to break the culture of refusal among all of our adolescent students, but particularly of our multiply–marginalized students, students like many of my undergraduates above, who are acutely aware that neither school nor their communities are behind them, supporting them as they struggle into adulthood.

As informed community members, however, we must be vigilant. If mainstream society appears to be increasingly unprepared for adolescents by not providing them the support systems they need, or simply by displaying their outright disdain for those adolescents who are not white and mainstream, we need to be increasingly "prepared" for them ourselves. That is, we need to be educated and educable as to what policies, both social and academic, affect adolescents and their schooling in our communities, and how we as community members can work to alter policies so that they, indeed, work to benefit all students.

For example, as New York State education officials attempted to put into place a new higher passing rate for the Regents exams that *all* students must take to graduate high school, community members joined educational leaders, including teachers and students, in protest. At issue was the fact that many of the rural and urban school districts that make up this upstate community (in particular) saw a large, and definable, increase in the number of students passing the Regents when the rate was at 55. As a matter of fact, the numbers were so heavily skewed in reflecting this, especially in the most remote rural and challenged urban schools, that it seems unlikely that any of these students would pass with the new, proposed higher percentage of 65. As a result of community members' reactions to school officials' compiling and presenting these data, one local paper reported that the Board of Regents was persuaded to at least consider a compromise—that of re–adjusting the passing rate to 60 (Rosenberg, 2001, B1, B4). Here, clearly informed community members sought to change what they saw as, at best, an uniformed decision by state policy makers and, at worst, a dangerous one proposed by the very officials designated to provide equal education for all.

Issues surrounding the education of the adolescent inmate population have also been covered more extensively by local and national newspapers. Managing "good" prisons is perceived, fundamentally, as a public safety issue first and foremost; yet, as educational findings funnel from the ivory towers through the media and to the community at large, community interest (and activism) has piqued. Led, perhaps, by a growing consensus among the media and policy makers that educating inmates leads to better outcomes when they leave prison, funders have re–opened their purses to entice new studies to better explore the issue.

For example, one such study concludes that inmates who receive an education while in prison are far less likely to return to prison within three years of their release so that, from a financial (rather than an educational) point of view, every dollar you spend on education, you save two dollars by avoiding the cost of re–incarceration. And a second study, funded by the philanthropist, George Soros, shows clearly that those who enroll and complete college classes while in prison found "even greater benefits" than those (presumably, adolescents) who just complete their GEDs.

What Can We Do as Teachers/as Parents/as Citizens of a Global, Diverse World?

The New York Times ("Queens Man," 2001) has recently reported that one of the two men accused of beating two Mexican migrant workers in Long Island has been convicted by a jury on two counts of attempted murder, assault, and aggravated harassment. The jurors were asked to consider that this defendant was in a rage from alcohol and drug abuse and that, therefore, his racism should be excused. It was an important message to send to the community as a whole, but especially, I believe, to the migrant community both in Long Island and in other parts of New York State and around the country. That message seems loud and clear: the search for equality and justice still rings true; the United States is still a place where there are possibilities for all.

There is, indeed, a danger since the horrific acts of terrorism conducted against this country on September 11, 2001, that we may see a backlash and a renewed fear of foreigners—of those who don't look like the mainstream—of those who don't speak English—of those who cannot succeed in traditional school settings—of those who by virtue of their poverty, or lack of opportunities, or immigrant status, may simply be different. But I believe that teachers, parents, and community activists like Stephanie and Colleen, who work tirelessly among those who are different—those who are multiply–marginalized—must continue the struggle. And this work may be most compelling among a group of students—adolescents—who in Ayers' (1997) words, begin the tumultuous journey into adulthood.

Whether or not as Sadovnik & Semel write (2002), multiply–marginalized students need, or benefit most from, a "different curricular and pedagogical approach" (p. 29), one thing seems crystal clear: their culture of refusal begs us to try, to engage, and to believe in the possibilities of all of our students. As we bring into our classrooms and into our lives the richness and diversity of their local literacies, we watch, I believe, a transformation, albeit perhaps just a small one: an insignificant one in the larger, global society in which we live, and yet one that carries with it, so much hope and potential. This, I hope, in the shadow of September 11, 2001, is our legacy.

REFERENCES

————. (1998). *School opening alert.* Boston, MA: National Coalition of Advocates for Students.

Alvermann, D. E. (1992). *Researching the literal: Of muted voices, secondary texts, and cultural representations.* Chicago, IL: National Reading Conference, Inc.

Andersen, K. & Jack, D.C. (1991). *Learning to listen: Interviewing techniques and analyses.* In Gluck, S.B. & Patai, D. (Eds.). Women's words: The feminist practice of oral history. London: Routledge.

Anyon, J. (1997). *Ghetto schooling: A political economy of urban educational reform.* New York: Teachers College Press.

Atwell, N.M. (1987). *In the middle.* Upper Montclair. NJ: Boyton/Cook.

Ayers, W. (2001). *To teach: The journey of a teacher.* NY: Teachers College Press.

Ayers, W. (1992). *Work that is real: Why teachers should be empowered.* In Hess, G. A. (Ed.), Empowering parents and teachers. Westport, CT: Bergin and Garvey.

Ayers, W. (1993). *The good preschool teacher.* New York: Teachers College Press.

Ayers, W. (1997). *A kind and just parent: The children of juvenile court.* Boston, MA: Beacon Press.

Belenky, M.F., Clinchy, B.M., Goldberger, N.R. & Tarule, J.M. (1986). *Women's ways of knowing: The development of self, voice, and mind.* New York: Basic Books.

Blake, B.E. (1992). *Talk in non–native and native English speakers' peer writing conferences: What's the difference?* Language Arts, 69, 604–610.

Blake, B.E. (1995). *Doing number 5: From process to cultural texts in an urban writing classroom.* Language Arts, 72, 396–404.

Blake, B.E. (1997). *She say, he say: Urban girls write their lives.* Albany, NY: State University of New York Press.

Blake, B.E. & Blake, R.W. (2002). *Literacy learning: A reference handbook.* Santa Barbara, CA: ABC–CLIO Publishing

Blake, R. W. (1990). *Whole language: Explorations and applications.* Urbana, IL: National Council of Teachers of English.

Blake, R. W. (1996). *Reader response: Toward an evolving model for teaching literature in the elementary grades.* The Language and Literacy Spectrum, 6, 39–44.

Boland, E. (1994). *In a time of violence.* New York: Norton.

Boyce, C. J. (1994). *For those behind bars, education is rehabilitation.* Minneapolis Star and Tribune, p. 1–2.

Boyce, C.J. (1995). *For those behind bars, education is rehabilitation.* University of Minnesota/Corrections Education Research Center: MN.

Brown, L.M. & Gilligan, C. (1992). *Meeting at the crossroads: Women's psychology and girls' development.* Cambridge, MA: Harvard University Press.

Calkins, L.M. (1983). *Lessons from a child.* Portsmouth, NH: Heinemann.

Calkins, L.M. (1986). *The art of teaching writing.* Portsmouth, NH: Heinemann.

Chomsky, N. (1957). *Syntactic structures.* The Hague: Mouton.

Classroom crackdown: Chicago tries tough approach to turn its schools around. (1998, April, 9). The Democrat & Chronicle. 1, 10.

Cohen, S., Pollowya, E., & Wallace, G. (1987). *Language arts: Teaching exceptional children.* Austin, TX: Pro Ed.

Covington, J. (1997). *The social construction of the minority drug problem.* Social Justice, 24, 4, 117–148.

Darder, A. (1991). *Culture and power in the classroom: A critical foundation for bicultural education.* New York: Bergin & Garvey.

Delpit, L. (1995). *Other people's children.* New York: The New Press.

Diaz, J., Trotter, R., & Rivera, V. (1989). *The effects of migration on children: An ethnographic study.* Harrisburg, PA: Pennsylvania Department of Education, Division on Migrant Education.

Domino, J. & Gersten, R. (1993). *Visions and revisions: A special education perspective on the whole language controversy.* RASE, July/August, 1–9.

Dryfoos, J. (1990). *Adolescents at risk.* New York: Oxford University Press.

Dyson, A. H. & Freedman, S.W. (1990). *On teaching writing: A review of the literature.* (Occasional Paper No. 20). Berkeley, CA: Center for the Study of Writing.

Educational Services for youth. (1998). *Statutory authority, Correction law,* 45(6); Education law 3202 (7). New York State.

Eisner, E. W. (1997). *The promise and perils of alternative forms of data representation.* Educational Researcher, 26, 6, 4–10.

Endless rows and hardship on black dirt farms: For migrant workers, the decades hardly change working or living conditions. (1996, July, 9). The New York Times. B1, B6.

Erickson, E. (1963). *Childhood and society.* New York: Norton.

Erickson, E. (1968). *Identity: Youth and crisis.* New York: Norton.

Faludi, S. (1999). *Stiffed: The betrayal of the American man.* New York: Morrow & Co.

Ferrell, J. (1997). *Youth, crime, and cultural space.* Social Justice, 24, 4, 21–38.

Ferrell, J. (1997). *Youth, crime, and cultural space.* Social Justice, 24, 4, 21–38.

Field, J. & Jardine, D. (1996). *Restoring the life of language to its original difficulty: On hermeneutics, whole language and authenticity.* Language Arts, 73, 255–259.

Fine, M. (1987). *Silencing in the public schools.* Language Arts, 64, 157–175.

Fine, M. (1991). *Framing dropouts.* Albany, NY: SUNY Press.

Fine, M. (1991). *Why urban adolescents drop into and out of public high school.* Teachers College Record, 393–409.

Fine, M. (1994). *Working the hyphens: Reinventing self and other in qualitative research.* In Denzin & Lincoln (Eds.), Handbook of qualitative research. Thousand Oaks, CA: Sage.

Fine, M. & Weis, L. (1998). *Crime stories: A critical look through race, ethnicity, and gender.* Qualitative Studies in Education, 11, 3, 435–460.

Fine, M. & Zane, N. (1991). *Being wrapped too tight: When low–income women drop out of high school.* Women's Studies Quarterly, XIX, 77–99.

Frankenberg, R. (1993). *The social construction of whiteness: White women, race matters.* Minneapolis: University of Minnesota Press.

Freire, P. (1986). *Pedagogy of the oppressed.* New York: Continuum Publishing.

Freud, S. (1978). *Basic works of Sigmund Freud.* Franklin Center, PA: The Franklin Library.

Garbarino, J. (1999). *Lost boys: Why our sons turn violent and how we can save them.* New York: Free Press.

Gee, J.P. (1996). *Social linguistics and literacies: Ideology in discourses.* London: Falmer.

Gere, A.R. & Abbott, R.D. (1985). *Talking about writing: The language of writing groups.* Research in the Teaching of English, 19, 362–381.

Gilbert, P. & Taylor, S. (1991). *Fashioning the feminine: Girls, popular culture, and schooling.* North Sydney, Australia: Allen & Unwin.

Gilbert, P. (1989). *Writing, schooling, and deconstruction: From voice to text in the classroom.* London: Routledge.

Gilligan, C. (1982). *In a different voice: Psychological theory and women's development.* Cambridge, MA: Harvard University Press.

Gilligan, C. (1990). *Teaching Shakespeare's sister: Notes from the underground of female adolescence.* In Gilligan, C., Lyons, N.P., & Hanmer, T. J. (Eds.), Making connections: The relational worlds of adolescent girls at Emma Willard School. Cambridge, MA: Harvard University Press.

Giroux, H.A. (1988). *Teachers as intellectuals: Toward a critical pedagogy of learning.* Granby, MA: Bergin & Garvey.

Give farmworkers a place at table of employee rights. (1998, March, 24). The Democrat & Chronicle, 7A.

Gluck, S.B. & Patai, D. (Eds.). (1991). *Women's words: The feminist practice of oral history.* London: Routledge.

Goodman, K. (1986). *What's whole about whole language?* Portsmouth, NH: Heinemann.

Graves, D. H. (1983). *Writing: Teachers and children at work.* Portsmouth, NH: Heinemann.

Graves. D. H. (1986). *What children show u about revision.* In Walshe, R.D. (Ed.), Donald Graves in Australia. Rosebery, NSW, Australia: Bridge Printery.

Greene, M. (1965). *The public school and the private vision: A search for America.* New York: Random House.

Gutnecht, B. (1991). *Transition in reading instruction: From a skills acquisition to whole language model.* Journal of Instructional Psychology, 18, 1–7.

Hall, S. H. (1999) *The troubled life of boys: The bully in the mirror.* (August, 22). The New York Times Magazine. Pp. 31–35.

Harding, S. (1987). *Feminism and social science issues.* Bloomington: Indiana University Press.

Heath, S. B. (1983). *Ways with words: Language, life, and work in communities and classrooms.* New York: Cambridge University Press.

Heath, S. B. & McLaughlin, M.W. (1993). *Identity and inner-city youth: Beyond ethnicity and gender.* New York: Teachers College Press.

Hechinger, F.M. (1993). *Schools for teenagers: A historic dilemma.* In Takanishi, R. (Ed.) Adolescence in the 1990's: Risk and opportunity. New York: Teachers College Press.

Heilbrun, C.G. (1988). *Writing a woman's life.* New York: Ballantine Books.

Hinojosa, D., & Miller L. (1984). *Grade level attainment among migrant farm workers in south Texas.* Journal of Educational Research, 77,6, 346–350.

Hollingsworth, S. (1992). *Learning to teach through collaborative conversation: A feminist approach.* American Educational Research Journal, 29, 373–404.

Hornberger, N.H. & Skilton-Sylvester, E. (1998). *Revisiting the continua of biliteracy: International and critical perspectives.* Paper presented at the Annual Meeting of the American Educational Research Association (AERA), San Diego, CA.

Hudelson, S. (1989). *Write on: Children writing in ESL.* Englewood Cliffs, NJ: Prentice Hall.

Hull, G. & Schultz, K. (2002). *School's out: Bridging out–of–school literacies with classroom practice.* New York: Teachers College Press.

Jaffee, A. (1993). *Involvement, detachment, and representation of Corsica.* In Brettell (Ed.), When they read what we write: The politics of ethnography. Westport, CT: Bergin & Garvey.

Jipson, J., Munro, P., Victor, S., Froude Jones, K., Freed Rowland, G. (1995). *Repositioning feminism and education: Perspectives on educating for social change.* Westport, CT: Bergin & Garvey.

Kaplan, L. J. (1984). *Adolescence: The farewell to childhood.* New York: Simon & Schuster.

Karier, C. Spring, J., & Violas, P. (1973). *Roots of crisis: American education in the twentieth century.* Chicago: Rand McNally.

Kell, C. (1997). *Literacy practices in an informal settlement.* In Prinsloo, M. & Breir, M. (Eds), The social uses of literacy: Theory and practice in South Africa. (pp. 235–256). Philadelphia, PA: John Benjamins Press.

Kincheloe, J. L. (1991). *Teachers as researchers: Qualitative inquiry as a path to empowerment.* London: The Falmer Press.

Kincheloe, J. L. (2001). *Getting beyond the facts: Teaching social studies/social sciences in the twenty–first century.* New York: Peter Lang Publishing.

Kirsch, G.E. (1999). *Ethical dilemmas in feminist research: The politics of location, interpretation, and publication.* Albany: State University of New York Press.

Kohlberg, L. & Kramer, R. (1969). *Continuity and discontinuity in child and adult moral development.* Human Development, 12, 93–120.

Kohlberg, L. (1981). *The philosophy of moral development: Moral stages and the idea of justice*. San Francisco: Harper & Row.

Kohlberg, L. (1987). *Child psychology and childhood education: A cognitive–developmental view*. New York: Longman.

Ladson–Billings, G. (1994). *The dreamkeepers*. San Francisco: Jossey–Bass.

Lewin, T. (1995). *Behind prison walls, poor reading skills also pose a barrier*. University of Minnesota/Corrections Education Research Center: MN.

Lewin, T. (2001, November 16). *Inmate education is found to lower risk of new arrest*. The New York Times, National, A18.

Lowe, D. & Lowe, S. (1992). *Whole language for at–risk readers*. Preventing school failure, 37, 14–21.

Martin, P. (1994). *Migrant farmworkers and their children*. U.S. Department of Education. Office of Educational Research and Improvement. ERIC Clearinghouse on Rural Education and Small Schools.

Martin, S.L., Gordon, T.E., & Kupersmidt, J.B. (1994). *Survey of exposure to violence among the children of migrant and seasonal farm workers*. Public Health Reports, 110, 3, 268–276.

Martin, S.L., Gordon, T.E., Kupersmidt, J.B. (1995). *Survey of exposure to violence among children of migrant and seasonal farm workers*. Public Health Reports, 110, 3, 268–276.

Mayor, F. (1999). Foreward. In Wagner, D.W., Venezky, R. L., & Street, B. V. (Eds.), *Literacy: An international handbook*. Boulder, CO: Westview Press.

Miller, R. (1990). *What are schools for: Holistic education in American culture*. Brandon, VT: Holistic Education Press.

Mumford, L. (1979). *Interpretations and forecasts: 1922–1972*. New York: Harcourt Brace.

New York State Department of Education (1995). *U.S. Census Bureau Report. New York State Migrant Education Department.*_____. *Certificate of Eligibility/Definition of Migratory Children*. Document # 950051.

News Article. (1997, August, 8) The New York Times, National, A16.

News Article. (1999, January, 1). The Democrat & Chronicle, 8A.

Noddings, N. (1992). *The challenge to care in schools*. New York: Teachers College Press.

Pappas, C.C. (1990). *An integrated language perspective in the elementary school: Theory into Action*. White Plains, NY: Longman.

Phelan, P., Davidson, A.L. & Yu, H.C. (1998). *Adolescents' worlds: Negotiating family, peers, and school.* New York: Teachers College Press.

Pleck, J. H. (1988). *1988 Survey of adolescent males.* Urbana-Champaign: University of Illinois.

Pollack, W. (1998). *Real boys: Rescuing our sons from the myths of boyhood.* NY: Henry Holt.

Queens man is convicted in L.I. attack on Mexicans. (December 13, 2001). The New York Times. Metro Section. D5.

Real, T. (1997). *I don't want to talk about it: Overcoming the secret legacy of male depression.* New York: Scribner.

Reyes, M. (1991). *A process approach to literacy instruction for Spanish–speaking students: In search of a best–fit.* In E.H. Hiebert (Ed.), Literacy for a diverse society: Perspectives, practices, and policies. New York: Teachers College Press.

Reyes, M. (1995). *Strawberry scam sharecropping revives exploitation of farm workers.* San Jose Mercury News, B6.

Rodby, J. (1992). *Appropriating literacy: Writing and reading in English as a second language.* Portsmouth, NH: Heinemann.

Rogers, A. (1993). *Voice, play, and a practice of ordinary courage in girls' and women's lives.* Harvard Educational Review, 63, 265–295.

Rosenberg, E. (2002, December 27). *Regents look at 60 score to pass.* The Democrat & Chronicle, 1B, 4B.

Sadovnik, A.R. & Semel, S. F. (2002). *Urban school improvement: A challenge to simplistic solutions to educational problems.* Educational Researcher, 30, 9, 27–32.

School opening alert (1998, July). National Coalition of Advocates for Students. p. 1.

Schubert, W. H. (1986). *Curriculum: Perspective, paradigm, and possibility.* New York: Macmillan.

Sengupta, S. (2001, March 9). *Pataki proposes changes in drug sentencing.* The New York Times, Metro, B4.

State University of New York. (1996). *Migrant Education Project. Teacher Handbook.* Brockport, NY: State University of New York.

Stein, N. Katz, S.R., Madriz, E. & Shick, S. (1997). *Losing a generation: Probing the myths and realities of youth and violence.* In Social Justice, 24, 4, 1–6.

Straus, M.B. (1994). *Violence in the lives of adolescents.* New York: Norton.

Street, B.V. (1995). *Social literacies: Critical approaches to literacy in development, ethnography, and education.* New York: Longman.

Street, B.V. (2001). *Introduction*. In Street, B.V. (Ed), Literacy and development: Ethnographic perspectives. London: Routledge.

Szwed, J. F. (1981). *The ethnography of literacy*. In Whiteman (Ed.), Writing: The nature, development, and teaching of written communication, part 1. Hillsdale, NJ: Erlbaum.

Takanishi, R. (Ed.) (1993). *Adolescence in the 1990's: Risk and Opportunity*. New York: Teachers College Press.

Traub, J. (2000). *Schools are not the answer: What no school can do*. (January).The New York Times Magazine. 52–57, 68, 81, 90, 91.

Trueba, Guthrie, & Au, K. (1981). (Eds.) *Culture and bilingual education: Studies in classroom ethnography*. Rowley, MA: Newbury House Publishers.

Upchurch, C. (1996). *Convicted in the womb: One man's journey from prisoner to peacemaker*. New York: Bantam Books.

Willinsky, J. (1990). *The new literacy: Redefining reading and writing in the schools*. New York: Routledge.

Willis, A. I. (1995). *Reading the world of school literacy: Contextualizing the experience of a young African–American male*. Harvard Educational Review, 65, 1, 30–49.